KEEPING
GLASGOW
IN STITCHES

Edited by

LIZ ARTHUR

Introduction by

CLARE HIGNEY

MAINSTREAM
PUBLISHING

EDINBURGH AND LONDON

First published in Great Britain 1991 by
MAINSTREAM PUBLISHING COMPANY (EDINBURGH) LTD
7 Albany Street
Edinburgh EH1 3UG

ISBN 1 85158 407 2 (paper)

A catalogue record for this book is available from the British Library

Designed by James Hutcheson and Paul Keir

Typeset in 12/14 Linotron Sabon
Printed in Great Britain by Butler & Tanner,
Frome

CONTENTS

ACKNOWLEDGMENTS

To the contributors Clare Higney; Malcolm Lochhead; Mark O'Neill; Liz Carnegie; Margaret Burniston; Libby McArthur and Eirene Houston; Liz Lochhead; Mrs J. Dreghorn; Marcella Evaristi; Roddy Forsyth; William Hunter; Joseph Farrell; Adam McNaughton; Jim McLean; and Dr Alastair Cameron, the Dept of Theatre, Film and Television Studies, University of Glasgow, for their willingness to meet impossible deadlines, and to the staff and pupils of Kelvinhaugh and St Marnock's schools for their continuing interest.

To Susan Green of NeedleWorks for her constant good humour and willingness to help; Walter Gilmour for sharing his knowledge and enthusiasm and Janey Buchan for selecting the work of her late husband. To Irene Woods; Elizabeth Bailey, Centre Manager for Princes Square; David Mullane; Debby Gee at Vidal Sassoon; Elizabeth Watson; Olive Rankin; Ruth Murphy; Hans van der Gryjp; Mr F. C. Buntin, the Shettleston Activity in Retirement Group; and Glasgow City Council Parks Department, all of whom have helped in many ways. Particular thanks go to Bill Arthur and the staff of Glasgow Museums, without whose encouragement and help this book would not have been possible.

For permission to reproduce their designs we thank Malcolm Lochhead; Sandi Kiehlmann; Lindi Richardson; and Malcolm McCormick; and photographers David Peace; Susan Scott; Christopher Nicoletti; Malcolm R. Hill; James Gillies; K. Inglis; Jane Carroll; Reg Allen; Diane Tammes; Ken Gillies; Neil Mackenzie Smith; Granville Fox. For permission to publish photographs from their collections we thank Springburn Museum Trust; Walter Gilmour; *Glasgow Herald*, D. C. Thomson and the University of Glasgow Theatre Archive. We appreciate the kindness of Liz Campbell, Margaret Burniston and Martha McPherson in allowing us to use their family photographs. We would also like to thank Cordelia Oliver for allowing us to reproduce the work of her late husband George Oliver.

We are indebted to the funders and sponsors who made the *Keeping Glasgow in Stitches* project possible: Glasgow City Council; Strathclyde Regional Council; *Glasgow Herald*; McGrigor Donald; The Warehouse; Benson Design Glasgow; BP Exploration; Liberty; The Scottish Daily Record and Sunday Mail (1986) Ltd; British Railways Board Community Unit; Clydesdale Bank PLC; Coats Leisure Crafts Group; various unions; The Queen's College; Madeira Threads (UK) Ltd; Pfaff (Britain) Ltd; Henry Milward & Sons Ltd; Mandors Fabric Retailers, Glasgow; Pod & Jois, Glasgow; Art Fabrics, Glasgow; Marji Leisurecraft of Bearsden; Twilleys of Stamford; ICI Paints Ltd; The Nelson-Atkins Museum; Freudenberg; Perivale-Guterman Ltd; and The Trades House, Glasgow.

Finally, but most importantly, our thanks go to the artists, workshop leaders and participants. They turned an idea into a reality and made 1990 a special year for all those associated with *Keeping Glasgow in Stitches*.

DIDN'T WE DO WELL!
(*David Peace*)

FOREWORD

Shortly after I arrived in Glasgow I saw a community banner project, conducted by NeedleWorks in the East End. I was so impressed with it that I wondered if it would be possible to expand the idea and make it city-wide, to make a Bayeaux tapestry of Glasgow life during its cultural year, serving both as a celebration and a record. I suggested to NeedleWorks that the Art Gallery and Museum could provide a base. I like the idea of things going on in museums – people doing things, not just looking at things – and the vast central hall of the Art Gallery and Museum, Kelvingrove, is ideal for this kind of activity.

I had no idea what it would take to bring such a project to fruition. Clare Higney did, and still she went on with it! A vague notion was transformed by NeedleWorks into brilliant reality. With superb organisational skills they orchestrated the talents of hundreds of people to produce what surely must be one of the largest and liveliest community arts projects in the world. The overall effect is stunning, as we learnt when we saw the banners hanging round the pillars in the Art Gallery. Visually so exuberant, they are also packed with wonderfully evocative detail, at times moving, at other times funny – pure Glasgow. People spent hours going round, poring over the banners, and bathing in their sumptuous colours and textures. And they were not just the people who'd made them! *Keeping Glasgow in Stitches* got everyone to participate. And that, I suppose, is its quality: its fundamental generosity of spirit.

JULIAN SPALDING
Director, Glasgow Museums

WORKSHOP IN
PROGRESS, THE MAIN
HALL IN THE ART
GALLERY AND
MUSEUM (*David Peace*)

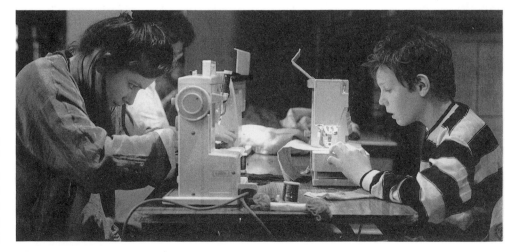

"THESE MACHINES
ARE MAGIC!"
LORRAINE DAVIN
AND AN
ENTHUSIASTIC
MACHINIST
(*David Peace*)

INTRODUCTION

'Come to Glasgow for a laugh, go away in stitches'

So goes an old Glasgow joke favoured by those who like to maintain the city's reputation for camaraderie and casualties. *Keeping Glasgow in Stitches*, an extraordinary community sewing project in 1990, Glasgow's year as European City of Culture, aimed to give that old joke a new meaning.

By the 1980s the city's hard-man image was wearing increasingly thin. Robbed of its heavy industry, beset with rising unemployment and poverty, Glasgow needed a new image to survive. When, at the tail end of the decade, the local authorities were successful in their bid to have Glasgow designated as European City of Culture 1990, the cynics had a field day. Glasgow as a City of Culture – you must be joking! The only culture Glasgow had, said the wags, was the one growing on the walls of the high-rise flats. *Keeping Glasgow in Stitches* was to show that culture was in everybody's hands – that, given the invitation, local people had the skill, imagination and enthusiasm to create a unique masterpiece capturing the spirit of their city, reaffirming what has always been Glasgow's strong sense of its own identity.

Created by NeedleWorks, a Glasgow-based community business, organised jointly by NeedleWorks and Glasgow Museums, and funded by Glasgow City Council, Strathclyde Regional Council and local and national businesses, *Keeping Glasgow in Stitches* involved over 600 people of all ages and abilities. Working together throughout 1990 they fashioned twelve 15-foot high banners, one for each month of the year, illustrating the people and the life of Glasgow. With an overall design by Malcolm Lochhead, Head of Design at Queen's College, Glasgow, and month by month designs commissioned from painters, cartoonists, textile artists and printmakers, *Keeping Glasgow in Stitches* became a unique fabric calendar celebrating the city with humour, poignancy, honesty and pride.

The initial response to the suggestion that NeedleWorks should join forces with Glasgow Museums to organise a participatory sewing project in the city's main museum was one of apprehension. Needle-Works is a community sewing business with a serious economic aim and a gregarious style. Working to create jobs and promote women's skills through the medium of banners and wall-hangings, it was fast winning a reputation for being innovative, and at times even witty, particularly in its local projects. The museum world was not known for its interest in vivacious activity. Its notion of a participatory sewing project would surely be one involving 'proper' ladies sitting in a docile circle making an inventory of civic buildings in meticulous cross-stitch. But while NeedleWorks was not brash in its approach, its style was definitely not docile. Workshops were cheery affairs with colourful heaps of fabric and busy activity – even laughter at times, and sometimes even raucous laughter! Was the museum world ready for an accessible and inclusive brand of community art which defied the stereotyped image of sewing as a gentlewoman's craft? Well, Glasgow's museums certainly were.

Julian Spalding is a believer in spring cleaning – not just dusting –

MRS GANDHI SHARES
HER EXPERTISE
(*David Peace*)

10

to brush the cobwebs off the public's view of galleries as silent monuments to worthy relics. He wanted to encourage imaginative (some said too imaginative) ways to a livelier public experience. *Keeping Glasgow in Stitches* was to become a project of mutual advantage but it was a risk. If NeedleWorks was wary of blunting its aims by crossing the establishment threshold, Glasgow Museums was equally nervous. What if the project was a shambles, the finished work an embarrassment? Could this young community business really deliver a masterpiece made by hundreds? For 1990 the risk on both sides seemed worth taking.

From the very beginning *Keeping Glasgow in Stitches* was a public project. Inspired by the opportunity for community arts to have a central place on Glasgow's cultural magic carpet, it transported local creativity and images from the back streets to the marbled main hall of the city's Art Gallery and Museum at Kelvingrove. There, for three days a week and the last Saturday of every month throughout the year, the public could watch the work unfold. They could wander round the tables at their ease, asking questions, pointing out local features to visiting friends, even getting involved themselves. The interest was so great that we had to set up a separate project, *Glimpses of Glasgow*, allowing hundreds of people to make 6-inch squares each showing their own sewn images of the city and thus managing to absorb the huge public enthusiasm into the scheme.

People came from the whole of Strathclyde Region, were of all backgrounds, cultures, ages and abilities. We made sure from the start that the feel of *Keeping Glasgow in Stitches* was relaxed and welcoming. The title was a vital trigger to this. We spent hours poring over dictionaries of quotations and the *Thesaurus*, trying to find the right phrase, with the right tone. To have called it *The Glasgow Tapestry* would have doomed it to an overworthy personality. *Keeping Glasgow in Stitches* had an air of appealing irreverence – well suited to Glaswegian humour. It attracted interest and, more significantly, involvement.

After the title came the themes. In a city such as Glasgow, rich in history, brimming with character, the choices were many, too many. There had to be some structure which made the choice of themes seem rational, if not logical. The first idea was a series of views out of and into windows by different people at different times. But somehow it seemed too clumsy, too contrived, and with sweet relief the idea of a

RENA ENCOURAGES A
VISITOR TO
EMBROIDER HER
*GLIMPSE OF
GLASGOW* (David Peace)

calendar came from nowhere and made perfect sense. The themes dropped snugly into this framework – the sales for January, politics for May, The Glasgow Fair for July. A review group, representing the widespread constituency of the project, was set up to complete the jigsaw – entertainment for December, the parks in spring for April, November, the month of remembrance. We worked with the trained eye of a professional designer for the first time – Malcolm Lochhead patiently accepting our demands for a scale big enough to depict a full-size human being, as well as many notions of the Clyde running through the whole work. He went to work with coloured card and rulers, colour charts and books on Glasgow and at a memorable meeting nervously unveiled an inspired and inspirational design into which detailed illustrative panels could be dropped with ease and effect.

Applications had to be made to the local authorities. In keeping with the uniqueness of the project, the first approach was made via an exquisite handmade little folder with images and text which was passed around and which, with the back-up of formal applications, won the project resources. A sponsorship campaign, championed by the *Glasgow Herald*, was launched. Letters were sent out to local and national manufacturers asking for goods in kind, for donations of fabric and thread, scissors and sewing needles. A local carpenter, Jack McPherson, was commissioned to make a giant sewing-box to house all that was needed for efficient use and easy storage. Artists were chosen, approached, encouraged and commissioned – some needed more encouragement than others to see the place that their creativity had in a sewing project. We wanted to involve not just people who liked to sew but all kinds of people so that the project truly represented the interests of the whole city. So we approached writers and photographers, historians and politicians, commercial companies and local colleges, the media and the men – deliberately creating reasons to ask for help with research and resources, to make contacts and encourage creative involvement. The response was always generous, sometimes unexpectedly magnanimous.

On 6 December 1989, with an invited audience of 250 participants, designers, press and companies, *Keeping Glasgow in Stitches* was launched. It was a baptism of fire for Susan Green, the project co-ordinator appointed only a fortnight before to take on the alarming role of keeping everybody happy over the next year. On a platform shared with Julian Spalding, Malcolm Lochhead and Liz Arthur, the assistant keeper of the Museum of Costume, who was the Museums' guardian of the project, Susan gamely answered questions on timetables and childcare, on techniques and tasks. With the media coverage and NeedleWorks' own mailshot to Embroiderers' Guild branches, local community groups, sewing classes and Social Services centres, the project became public and the deluge of enquiries began.

There were hundreds of offers of help – from people who wanted to come and sew; from companies keen to donate fabric; from groups like the Glasgow Lace Group and the Scottish Handicraft Circle offering the support and skills of their members. Potential participants were all sent questionnaires, asking what day and month they would like to work, what techniques they knew or wanted to learn. Packages and boxes began to arrive from companies – sewing-machines from Pfaff, a giant tuck box of all kinds of practical and exotic delights from Coats Leisure Crafts, needles and thimbles from Milwards, Vilene from Freudenberg and letters from others – Madeira Threads, Rowenta Irons, asking us to tell them what we would like.

As public interest grew and the number of participants soared we had to create a rota system. Changing monthly teams of stitchers were mixed by us into a dangerous cocktail of different ages, experience and personalities. The stimulus was to be social as well as creative! We gave some months what we called an emphasis group – mixed cultures for February, people from Springburn in March, Embroiderers' Guild members for April, children in July and men in September. This allowed us to contact specific groups and encourage their involvement. Some needed to be welcomed because they were less confident, others had creative skills that the project wanted to reflect – like the wide-ranging textile skills of the Embroiderers' Guild members or the exquisite hand work of the Asian embroiderers.

Sharing skills, ideas, problem solving and interpretation was a key factor of the whole project. Everyone had an equal contribution to make and we designed each banner deliberately to have its own separate identity, distinct mood and different techniques so that none could be compared, technically, with another. It was not a sewing competition but a creative project and each month's group had to be satisfied with their own creative efforts. Because of this we insisted, despite pressure, on not showing the banners until the end of the year apart from the first one, the January Sales. This was to ensure that the banners and the groups who made them shared the same moments of glory and that each banner would be seen as a vital part of a whole.

On 10 January at 8 a.m., armed with sewing-machines, baskets of fabric and boxes of thread, Susan Green and I nervously unpacked the ingredients of *Keeping Glasgow in Stitches* under the suspicious eyes of the security staff. BBC Radio 4 was there, recording the first day for what became a piece about the whole project at the end of the year. As sewing-machines were connected up and extra chairs sought, Beatty Rubens from the BBC asked what I hoped for the project. "That it will work," I said with failing faith that the museum world really *was* ready for the whir of a dozen sewing-machines. An elderly couple passed by and seeing participants' coats hung on rails and tables heaped with fabric asked, "What time does the jumble sale begin?" The phrase 'lowering the tone' crept unwillingly into my head and my heart sank. Maybe there was something to be said for meticulous cross-stitch after all. By 11 a.m. order reigned. There was a gentle but unobtrusive hum of sewing-machines and conversation, a constant flow of interested and delighted visitors – including museum staff – and school parties were poring over the designs and people taking information away for their mothers, daughters, even their husbands – "He's always been a keen sewer, you know." *Keeping Glasgow in Stitches* was off to a great start.

And so it continued for its three days a week and last Saturday of every month with the momentum of interest and activity unabated. Workshop leaders were employed for different months, all working with committed and intense creativity. Lesley Evans, booked to run the March workshop, proved to be a miracle worker, organising calm and contentment out of the potential chaos of new people and new creative challenges. She stayed to work on another four of the banners. Then, of course, the artists who had designed the various months became involved in the different workshops – advising, helping, explaining. Participants got used to the healthy irritations of any collective project when the scissors go missing and your chair suddenly disappears and practised patience and diplomacy with good will. They also took up easy residence in the marbled hall uninhibited by public curiosity, even inviting it, explaining the project and showing work-in-progress with pride.

Each month had its own atmosphere, its own stories, and you will find these in the book's different chapters. But the whole project had its own spirit of affection and application which won it the regard of the public. On 16 December *Keeping Glasgow in Stitches* was unveiled to an audience of 750 people seated on cushions in the main hall of the Art Gallery and Museum. The event started and ended with the 'Song of the Clyde', and in between there were 12 moments of anticipation, entertainment and applause as each banner was revealed in its own spotlight to the accompaniment of words and music presented by a group of professional musicians and pensioners, writers and school-children, singers and song-writers.

To the end, *Keeping Glasgow in Stitches* remained a unique community project, truly made in that well-known phrase: for the people, by the people and with the people. If there had been one overriding aim it was to surprise. To surprise visitors to the Museum by the unusual sight of creative activity; to surprise participants by how much talent they had, how much at ease they felt so quickly with each other and with a curious public watching over them; to surprise artists with how effectively their work could be interpreted into fabric and thread; to surprise the public with the sight of a man sewing, children spinning or words emerging from a computerised sewing-machine. Most of all to surprise everyone with the quality of what was created – the splendour and emotional appeal of these huge tactile evocations of Glasgow life.

The impact was more than we could have hoped for. People were not just surprised but amazed, enthralled. Even the world-weary journalists were moved:

> The 12 tapestries . . . are in place in the main hall and they are wonderful. I know that they represent the work of hundreds of people over the year but I hadn't expected to be moved to tears . . . This work transcends craft. In 100 years time people will look at these and they will know who we were and what we wanted.
>
> Ian Black, *The Bulletin*, January 1991

> There appears to be no feeling parts that the needle can't touch. In the night-on-the-town panel a red sunset saddens on the sullen surface of the Clyde's harbour with a magic that the city's famed paintbox would need genius to match . . . At the unveiling of the riches of *Keeping Glasgow in Stitches* there were strong men who wept.
>
> William Hunter, *Glasgow Herald*, 18 December 1990

How do we quantify the success of *Keeping Glasgow in Stitches*? It could be measured in practical terms, in the paid employment and artistic fees it provided to the local people whose talents are too often underused and undervalued. Or it might be seen in cultural terms, in the effectiveness of partnering a museum with a creative community organisation and pooling not just resources but mutual needs to offer the public a richer experience. But the most potent success must be seen in human terms, in the life-long friendship it forged between participants, the confidence and satisfaction it brought to those who took part, in the feelings it stirred in the people who saw the work being created with intimate affection by local people and finally as a work that transcends language and local culture to speak to others as clearly as it does to Glaswegians. When the banners went to Rostov on Don in the Soviet Union the community made, in secret, a 13th banner as a gift to the people of Glasgow. Their wonderful gift echoed the generosity of Glasgow's own people who gave the city the priceless gift of their time, talent and unflagging enthusiasm for *Keeping Glasgow in Stitches*.

CLARE HIGNEY
Creative Director, NeedleWorks

JANUARY

Sandi Kiehlmann studied Embroidery and Woven Textiles at Glasgow School of Art and now combines teaching with freelance work. Her design evolved from sketching in Glasgow shops.

JANUARY

The Sales

We must imagine that the banners are rather like the 12 pages of a calendar. The first begins with the opening seconds of the new year and the last ends as the bells ring out the old.

At the top of the January banner it is a crystal clear winter night and a pale sequinned moon hangs in a patchwork sky studded with glittering glass-bead stars. Silhouetted against the sky is a ghostly sailing ship. It symbolises Glasgow's history of trade with foreign countries. It also shows Glasgow's strong links with shipbuilding and the Clyde. The ship on which this design is based is to be found on top of the old Merchants' House in Bridgegate: there is another very similar ship-shaped weather vane on the dome of the new Merchants' House in George Square.

The ship is created in stiff black silk and if you look closely you will see that the fabric is pleated and stitched to suggest the planks of the wooden hull. The ship sits atop the map of the world as seen from above the North Pole. Near the centre, marked by a red blob, is Britain, with Glasgow at the heart of Europe as European City of Culture in 1990. The map is overlaid with several layers of aqua-coloured tulle suggesting the tidal movements of the oceans.

Each of the 12 banners has an inner image. This image continues and develops the principal theme and in each case is designed by a different artist or group. January's was designed and supervised by Sandi Kiehlmann, a textile artist who specialises in machine embroidery. It was a conscious decision at the outset that each banner should have a predominant technique or approach. Sandi spent a great deal of time drawing and photographing the aspects of the January sales that we all know and love. You will encounter all the 'types' that one bumps into. There are the glamorous girls trying on party frocks, while over in the shoe department the twins in matching red outfits are eyeing up the bargains. (Sandi's observations of the orange, yellow and green

MAKING WAVES

shoes is sharp and accurate and, of course, highly amusing.) There, too, is the harassed mother with a push-chair containing a wean protected by a plastic cover and that arch enemy of sale-goers, the old dearie with the shopping trolley guaranteed to clip your ankles.

The crowds are hurrying along well wrapped up against wind and the inevitable rain and armed with umbrellas. Centre front is the typical Glasgow couple. Their faces have been created in three-dimensional, solid machine-stitchery. They are somewhat wind-blown and lashed by the torrent of glass raindrops. If you listen very carefully you can almost hear her mutter to him, "Ma feets aff me!" Both sets of feet and legs were added later in the year when we became more confident about breaking the edge of the inner image. The couple have bought something at the sales, hence the carrier-bag, but we will never know what. However, we can see a copy of the *Glasgow Herald* sticking out of the bag. Each of the banners was sponsored by a different organisation whose logo is incorporated in the design starting with the familiar *Glasgow Herald*.

On 4 January the first group met in NeedleWorks' own workshop. These 40 people, who had never met, had three days before they took up residence in the Art Gallery and Museum's main hall. They had the unenviable task of learning how to do machine-embroidery, as well as using this technique to create the showpiece of the year's project. They had to set the tone, the quality and the mood of *Keeping Glasgow in Stitches*, all in three days. There was the pensioner from Stranraer who had to be up at 6 a.m. to arrive in time; a group of young mothers from Robroyston who had just begun to learn hand-stitching in a NeedleWorks' project a few months earlier; a group of young trainee machinists from Springburn College; members of the Embroiderers' Guild and children from St Denis's Primary in Bridgeton. This eclectic group set to work with enthusiasm.

They experimented with various effects on the latest computerised sewing-machines donated by Pfaff. Amidst the "How do you . . . I'll never be able to . . . Could somebody please show me how to . . .?", samples were made as well as coffee and friendships. Richard Keir, the guardian angel of the sewing-machine, whizzed around rethreading here, reprogramming there, connecting leads and coaxing old machines into life.

By the time the group moved to the Art Gallery they seemed like

JILL McOWAT AND
ISOBEL CAVEN KEEP
THE WORLD IN
STITCHES

old hands, only too happy to show off the art of machine-embroidery. And the whirr of ten sewing machines did not intrude, as we had feared, on the quietude of the central hall, nor did the hum of discussion or the occasional shriek as someone held up a scrap of fabric questioningly to be told "Put that back, that's Iceland!"

The backgrounds of all the banners are made in patchwork. The different sized patches are mainly cotton, which readily accepts dye, and each banner is based on a particular coloured fabric, tie-dyed in a range of tones which is linked to the colours of the preceding and following months. This provides subtle changes of hue from one banner to the next and creates textural interest. The group met once a month in the wet laboratory of The Queen's College to dye the fabrics. On returning to the Art Gallery no detective work was needed to work out the colour range of the next banner: one glance at our tinted hands was enough.

However, the patchwork technique also gave different groups of people the chance to work on the task of putting the patches together, which demanded great accuracy. Arranged in strips, they were sewn on to a canvas backing strong enough to support the weight of all the surface work, some of which is very heavy. By May we had background-making down to a fine art – a total of 7 metres of fabric was needed for the 600 patches on each banner. Student priests came in to

make their 6-inch squares, and a group from Auchentoshan Adult Training Centre for the mentally handicapped came for a day and stayed for a year. They arrived faithfully every week.

The scene of creativity which the group presented delighted everyone. STV, BBC and German television all came to film, photographs were taken, newspaper and magazine articles appeared and all those involved were encouraged knowing that their efforts were so newsworthy. Indeed, when a Welsh television crew came they were amazed to find a Welsh speaker they could interview.

On the first Saturday of the project – the last of the month – the main hall was as busy as the January sales themselves. There was a tumble of children jostling to choose threads for their *Glimpses of Glasgow*. Four-year-old Donna turned out an exceptionally creative ice-cream cone, while Bhadra Meatha introduced others to fibre painting. But the moment when the completed top of the January panel was held aloft was memorable. The crowds gathered round and the participants fairly glowed with satisfaction. They had to wait until February when the final work was assembled to see its awesome scale and to realise the splendour of the work. And when the banner was at last hoisted over the balcony, friends and partners were there to photograph the proud moment.

"One down, only 11 to go . . . Whose idea was this anyway?"

Right SANDI KIEHLMANN LENDS ENCOURAGEMENT *Left* DRAWINGS FROM SANDI'S SKETCHBOOK

MASTER MACHINIST
RICHARD KEIR AT
WORK

REEAH ABERCROMBIE
BECOMES OBSESSED
WITH MACHINE-
EMBROIDERY

SHOPPING
Liz Arthur

Shopping has long been an important part of Glasgow life, whether the everyday kind of 'going the messages', or the special dressed-up foray into the city centre. It is a social event, an integral part of city life providing opportunities to meet friends, to chat to strangers, to look and be looked at.

Even in the 18th century shops and trade played an important role in the economic development of the city. Every Glasgow schoolchild learns of the city's merchant adventurers and the tobacco, sugar and rum trades. Few are aware that the ships sailing for America and the West Indies also carried in their holds stockings, boots, gloves, hats, leather breeches, fabrics, glassware, pottery and tools. This demand by the colonists gave rise to important manufacturing industries which greatly enhanced the prosperity of the city. In turn this encouraged the local demand for better quality, and more fashionable and more varied goods. So the shops developed until by the early 20th century there were many huge department-stores in Argyle, Buchanan and Sauchiehall streets.

Glasgow's shops attracted people from miles around (even Edinburgh). They came to look for that special outfit, or just to have a day out. The Barrows provided second-hand goods, cheap tea-sets and curtains, and best of all, entertaining patter. There was something for everyone.

By the 1950s Sauchiehall Street reigned supreme, home to Copland & Lye, Pettigrew & Stephens, Dalys and Trérons, as well as many smaller, specialist shops such as Art Fabrics, not to mention all the exclusive fashion outlets. Many women remember gazing at the discreet window displays of Grieve and Murielle but never daring to venture over the thresholds. This was still the time when customers received individual, unhurried attention in gracious surroundings. Seated on a chair by the glass counter with your elbow resting on a cushion the sales assistant would help you to try on gloves, each item being carefully returned to its glass-fronted drawer afterwards. Appointments could be made for special fittings and some stores offered a telephone sales service with goods delivered by van the same day whenever possible.

Argyle Street with its large emporia was not as well thought of by middle-class shoppers, but was the favourite haunt for many and provided a rich hunting ground at sale time. People would catch the first train to Glasgow in the hope of finding a real bargain, perhaps pots and pans in Lewis's or bed linen from Arnotts. Everyone tried to have a little extra money just in case something proved irresistible, and there was always that queue before opening time. And why did it always seem to rain? At nine o'clock the doors would open and decorum was forgotten as sales assistants were swept aside in the rush for bargains.

Later there would be time to relax and take stock in a tea-room somewhere. Miss Buicks, Craigs, Cranstons and Reids offered a wide choice of goodies, or there were always the tea-rooms in the big stores. Copland's had an orchestra on the balcony, and waitresses in black dresses and white aprons served under the watchful eye of the head waitress who knew all the regulars. The tables were small and there was nothing fancy, but the white linen was crisp and the waitresses friendly. Many people have childhood memories of these places and the fascinating vacuum tubes which sent money to the cash department and returned with a clatter and bump to dispense the change and receipt.

Department-store tea-rooms and restaurants were often used to show the latest fashions as well, with models parading around the tables. But most important were the annual autumn shows. Copland's introduced three daily parades in 1947 – the morning and afternoon ones costing 5/- (25p), with tea included and the evening one 3/6 (17½p), with the week's proceeds all going to charity. The fashions shown included luxury goods by top designers such as Schiaparelli and Balmain and items brought straight from Paris. Whitneys, the furriers in Buchanan Street, included:

> . . . an evening-dress of French silk net falling in a deep fish tail with chartreuse roses cunningly placed in the folds, [which] was sheer elegance. Its price – 350 guineas – stopped the show.
>
> *Women's Wear News*, 16 October 1947

Some stores bought abroad to retain a form of exclusiveness, but there could have been few Glaswegians who could afford 350 guineas for an

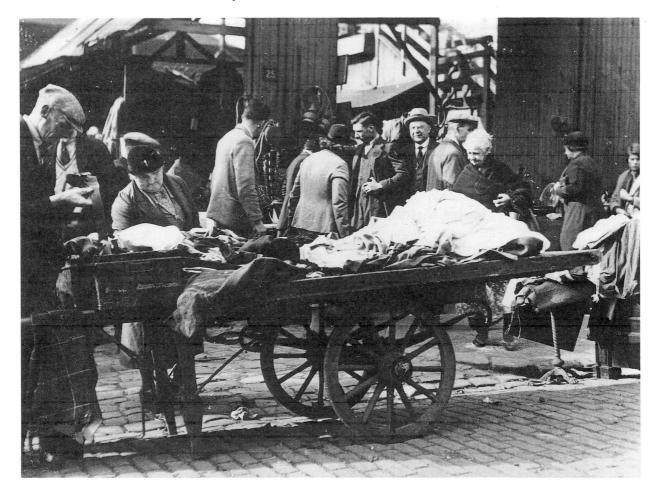

evening-dress. This would be a year's wages for many people and equivalent to about £3,600 today.

This was the Indian summer of the independent department-store, and the decline which had started in the 1920s continued despite attempts to attract new customers. Copland & Lye began publishing a bi-monthly magazine in 1950 and were the first firm to secure a 15-minute programme on Scottish Television in April 1959 to celebrate the modernisation of the store. Many others tried to adapt by introducing concessionary shops on their premises or by opening boutiques to cater for the young, but it was mainly the loyalty of old customers which enabled them to remain open. Their staid, middle-class image did not appeal to the mass market and they lost out to the modern, less formal chain-stores and supermarkets offering cheaper prices and faster

A VIEW OF THE BARROWS BY MR MORGAN, 1939, WHO BOUGHT THE TARTAN TREWS DRAPED OVER THE HANDLE

service. Added to this was the huge burden of rates. In Sauchiehall Street these were higher than London's Oxford Street and Lewis's, Scotland's largest store, had to pay out more than £1 million each year. Many stores passed out of the hands of the founding families through mergers and take-overs. Fifteen stores became part of the House of Fraser until by 1959 this most successful company had 60 branches employing 20,000 people. By 1970 House of Fraser, with its flagship Harrods, was the largest department-store chain in Britain, while the last of the Sauchiehall Street stores, Copland's, closed in 1971, Trérons had a serious fire in 1986 and only Watt Bros now remains.

It is ironic that the main cause of the demise of the independent department-store was an idea originated in nearby Greenock. The multiple chain-stores were begun by Fleming Reid Mills in 1881 when they began to establish their Scotch Wool Shops throughout the country. Chain-stores such as Marks & Spencer, who opened their 'Fancy Goods Bazaar' in Argyle Street in 1924, and the Dutch firm C & A, who opened eight years later, were able to centralise their buying on a countrywide basis. This, together with their rapid turnover of stock, enabled them to offer goods at cheaper prices which attracted a wider clientele who by the 1950s had more money to spend.

This desire to keep prices low and to speed up service gave rise to the main shopping innovation of the 20th century, self-service. It also created uniformity and blandness as identical chain-stores appeared in every town high street. In reaction, boutiques began to spring up selling, to the sound of pop music, the kind of goods demanded by the young, only to flourish and die and be replaced overnight by others.

Recently newer multiple chain-stores have taken advantage of the nostalgic elements in interior design and carefully cultivate a more personal atmosphere in smaller shops. They use lots of wood and metal fittings to create an image of quality, harking back to an earlier time, but without its formality, and without losing the convenience of modern shopping methods. With the development of expensive specialist shopping malls such as Princes Square, with its food court and events space, and the St Enoch Centre, with its skating rink, a new era of leisure shopping is with us. Some things have not changed. The buskers are there in even greater numbers and diversity, enlivening the pedestrian areas of the city centre and delighting the shoppers, and people still dress up to go shopping and bored partners still wait patiently outside.

THE BARROWS IN JUNE 1991. THE TARTAN TREWS HAVE BEEN RECYCLED

"CAN I HELP YOU, MODOM?" MISS BLACK THE STOCKING BUYER CHATS TO CUSTOMERS IN HER REVAMPED DEPARTMENT, COPLAND & LYE, APRIL 1959

WEATHERING THE STORM OF THE SALES (*Glasgow Herald*)

COPLAND'S SALE
ADVERTISEMENT,
1949

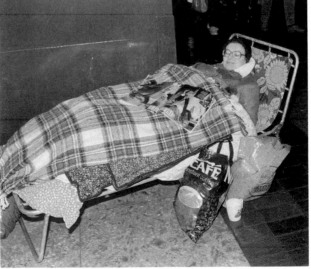

ELIZABETH
PETTIGREW IS
DETERMINED TO BE
FIRST IN THE QUEUE
FOR FRASER'S SALE,
1984 (*Glasgow Herald*)

HOPEFUL BARGAIN
HUNTERS, LEWIS'S,
1986 (*Glasgow Herald*)

SUCCESS, BUT NO
ONE'S TOLD HIM HE
HAD TO QUEUE FOR
PLUGS (*Glasgow Herald*)

SALES RUSH, C & A,
1983 (*Glasgow Herald*)

COPLAND'S
"YOUNG FASHION SHOP"
Opens to-day

THE pride of Copland's—this new
department for the 15's to early
20's—the pride of youth. Suits, Sports Outfits, Blouses,
Skirts, Formal and Informal Frocks—they are all chosen
especially to suit the style and purse of younger customers.

COPLAND & LYE LTD. • SAUCHIEHALL STREET • GLASGOW

COPLAND'S NEW
FASHION
DEPARTMENT, 1952

PRE-CREDIT CARD
SHOPPING RECEIPTS

MUSIC WHILE YOU
SHOP, JUNE 1991

FEBRUARY

Lorraine Davin studied
Embroidery and Woven
Textiles at Glasgow School
of Art. Her design and
practical experience
enabled the participants to
realise their ideas for this
panel.

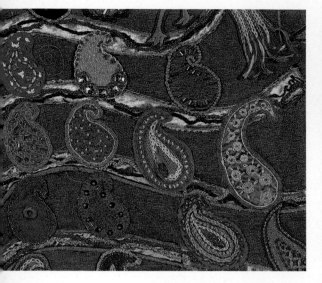

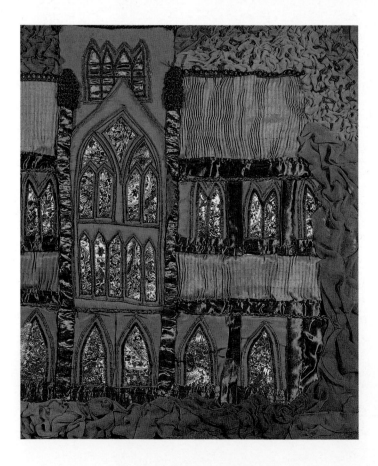

FEBRUARY
The Paisley Pattern

The aim of this banner is to remind people of the Asian origins of the Paisley motif and the cultural connections between East and West. Thus, the upper section of the banner illustrates this multicultural aspect through references to other religions which have enriched the spiritual life of the city.

The cathedral church of Saint Mungo, the patron saint of Glasgow, has been important to the development of the city and life revolved around it until the Reformation. The construction of this sewn cathedral is probably no less complex than the original! The green copper roof is of pleated fabric and the grey sharkskin stonework is cut away to reveal a beautiful multi-coloured and gold print beneath which gives the effect of stained glass lit from within.

The dome of the city mosque is represented in patchwork, painstakingly outlined with gold kid, while a Star of David representing the Jewish faith is couched into the branches of the tree which is central to the city's coat of arms.

Above this are the words 'The Clyde made Glasgow and [continued in March] Glasgow made the Clyde'. These words highlight another linking feature in the design. Along the top of each banner is a line of patchwork and stitchery symbolising the River Clyde flowing through the city. The Clyde is so important to Glasgow's history that a piece of work celebrating the city's life would have been incomplete without it. This simple 12-inch-wide strip gave the participants the opportunity to show off their skills creating the effects of light on water: dark and moody in January, bright and sparkly in July and reflecting the setting sun in October.

The large tree of the inner banner represents the Tree of Life and is based on an Indian symbol. The design was a collective effort between the Castlehead ladies of Paisley and Asian embroideresses from the International Flat who began their task in December 1989, visiting each other to discuss and agree the imagery and technique. It was decided that pairs of leaves in the form of the Paisley pine or cone pattern should be used. This motif is known worldwide and although its origins are obscure it can be traced to the decorative arts of Turkey, India and Persia. The motif as we know it came to Europe from Kashmir where it is known as the *būtā*. These leaves are worked in many different techniques, including traditional Asian methods using silks, sequins, beads and shisha glass.

Perched on the end of each branch is an exquisite exotic bird – again in an astonishing array of techniques – while sitting at the top is a gilded bird in a nest containing an egg represented by the Chinese Yin-Yang symbol. Yin is negative, dark and feminine, Yang is positive, bright and masculine. When they combine they maintain the harmony of everything in the universe. It has also been suggested that this, too, may have provided the inspiration for the Paisley motif. At the base of the tree is the skyline of Paisley town which in the 19th century became

CONSTRUCTION
WORK ON THE
CATHEDRAL

34

THIS LATE-16TH,
EARLY-17TH-
CENTURY INDIAN
BRONZE SCULPTURE
OF THE TREE OF LIFE
WAS USED AS THE
DESIGN SOURCE. THE
NELSON-ATKINS
MUSEUM OF ART,
KANSAS CITY,
MISSOURI (*Nelson Fund*)

IRENE WOODS
BUILDING THE
PAISLEY SKYLINE

And opposite
BIRDS OF A FEATHER:
THE FINE ART OF
BEADING

the centre of the shawl industry which was to make such widespread use of the *būtā* motif.

The horizontal maroon and grey silk strip represents the River Cart flowing through Paisley – specially woven by Sarah Sumsion using the ikat technique. This is an Indonesian technique which involves careful and exact tie-dyeing of the warp threads before they are put on to the loom.

Under the roots of the tree are all manner of exotic insects and strange creepy crawlies. Some of the beetles are of quilted black lamé with wings of vivid cerise and magenta velvet. Finally there are some large Paisley motifs containing images important to Paisley itself. One has the coat of arms of the town, another the house of Robert Tannahill, Paisley's famous weaver-poet, while one is dedicated to St Mirren, the local football team. The other shapes contain examples of different techniques and, of course, one reveals the identity of the sponsor, McGrigor Donald.

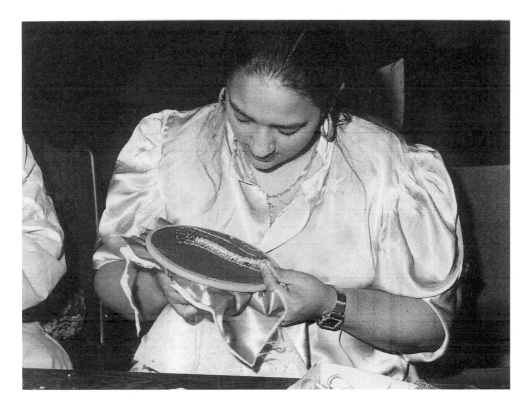

The workshops during February were like an Aladdin's cave of lustrous threads, shot silks, gleaming beads and metallic braids. People from India, Pakistan, Brazil and Chile were joined by mentally handicapped young adults from Hampden School and the children from Kelvinhaugh Primary School, who had made their own paper Tree of Life. Over 70 people took part, helped by Lorraine Davin. So many beautiful leaves and birds were created that a second banner had to be created to accommodate them all and this now hangs in the Castlehead Church, Paisley.

Glimpses of Glasgow continued unabated. Sergeant Graham came in to sew his 6-inch square for the Year of Road Safety and found himself the next day's pin-up in the *Glasgow Herald*. A glutton for punishment, he came back for more and ended up as a stalwart of *Keeping Glasgow in Stitches* and a member of NeedleWorks. Twenty-four arts and crafts teachers arrived from Stirling. Stuart Hopps, the choreographer, came to do his bit and as a welcome the portrait of him worked by John Byrne, now in the collection of Glasgow Museums, was specially hung for the day. The Museums' photographers became more and more used to the sudden calls to action. As recorders of the project they uncomplainingly captured its life as it unfolded month by month.

There were special moments of admiration. The private dinner for the Arts Minister, Richard Luce, started the ball rolling and then the visiting delegates from the Conference on International Arts saw the January banner being hung for the first time and a display of the work in progress on the February panel. This display was moved to the Citizens Theatre at the beginning of March for HM The Queen's visit to the inauguration of the 1990 cultural celebrations. The Queen met some of the February participants and received a framed textile of four *Glimpses of Glasgow*. This was presented by John Paul Carbery aged nine from St Denis's Primary School on behalf of Strathclyde Regional Council, an event commemorated in the March banner.

MAKING BEETLES AND ROOTS UNDER THE GUIDANCE OF WORKSHOP LEADER LORRAINE DAVIN

THE PAISLEY PATTERN
Clare Higney

Glasgow is an immigrant city, a city of many cultures. Italian ice-cream cafés are tucked in amongst Indian and Chinese restaurants, Asian fabric shops are next door to designer boutiques. The mosque graces the southern skyline as stylishly as Templeton's old carpet factory, heavily disguised as The Doge's Palace in Venice, stands in the East. The Irish came with the potato famine, the Gaels with the Clearances. Jewish immigrants from Central and Eastern Europe, Poles, Lithuanians, smaller groups of Ugandan, Chilean and Vietnamese refugees all settled in the city and made their own impression on its culture. In recent years people from Pakistan, India and China have made Glasgow their home and added to its richness.

Pulling the threads of these diverse communities together is a slow,

And over
JEAN LEADER MAKES
A LACE PAISLEY
MOTIF

39

at times painful process. Glaswegians have always had an appetite for the food of other lives and, not surprisingly, it was in the cafés, restaurants and delicatessens that tastes were most easily shared. In community life, in the social, political, religious and artistic ways of life, the sharing of experiences took longer and still needs positive encouragement.

So it was that in 1989 NeedleWorks established Mixed Threads, a project which aimed to bring together women of different cultures to share ideas, techniques and creativity. Through meeting the representatives of different groups and publicising information in four languages, NeedleWorks found enough support to organise the first Mixed Threads sewing project. Meeting in the International Flat, with the invaluable help of Mrs Ghandi and Jaya Verma, a group of Asian, African, South American and white Scottish women started to create a collective toran (welcome hanging). The services of the interpreter proved unnecessary as people communicated through their enthusiasm for sewing, teaching one another new ways of embroidering. With the toran in the making, another group of younger girls met in the

PAISLEY BUDDIES

Southside to work on a small fashion collection. They gave new life to old traditions with a *shalwar kamez* (woman's trousers and tunic) decorated with a castellated hem of bright shisha mirror work.

When a group of women from Paisley, with the keen encouragement of Irene Woods, asked if they could become involved with *Keeping Glasgow in Stitches* it seemed logical to connect them with the Mixed Threads group and make a contemporary link between the women of Paisley and the women of Asia. It was the Paisley weaving industry which, in the 19th century, had hijacked the symbol of the unfurling date-palm leaf from the Kashmiri craftsmen. Imitating the woven shawls which took one person six months to make, the Paisley mills produced a cheaper and more extensive range of shawl designs. Not only did Paisley take over the trade in shawls but also marketed the motif as its own with 'Paisley Pattern' becoming a household name. The motif was the source of Paisley's expanding prosperity, and the success in manufacture led to other companies setting up production in Paisley, amongst them Coats, then the thread manufacturers. By investing in design and creating an endless variety of colour and pattern, the Paisley shawl became a product line which, as they say, ran and ran.

It seemed appropriate to bring together a group that would trace the pattern back to its Asian origins, for there had been an ancient connection, too, between East and West in that the motif had passed from Babylonian culture into the imagery of both Celtic and Indian arts. While the shape of the leaf had lost definition in the Celtic complexities of swirls, it remained true to its form in the weavings and paintings of Asia. The teardrop, tadpole or leaf shape was a symbol of fertility, of new beginnings, and it was exciting to feel that in the making of the February banner, based on a Tree of Life design, a group

COMMEMORATIVE
CLOTH, 1887,
HYDERABAD, SINDH

42

of different cultures would intermix their cultural images to make a
new fusion, a symbol of their shared creativity reflecting the harmony
of the Yin-Yang sign. In the leaves the women sewed tiny images of
worship and work – a tatting shuttle, a lotus flower, a piece of knitting
– using the stitches of their different cultures and learning from one
another about mirror work or lace making. It was a new and rich
exchange.

Mixed Threads still continues, with projects both in Glasgow and
in Edinburgh. The NeedleWorks banners created for the summer of
1990 for Princes Square shopping centre in Glasgow used the structure
of a toran and involved women from the Mixed Threads group, now

EMBROIDERED
SHAWL

TORAN
(*David Peace*)

working in a paid capacity. Making the diverse cultures visible is a prime aim of the project. For the 1991 International Women's Day, a huge but delicate batik mobile was hung in the stairwell of the City Chambers in Edinburgh as an impressive display of women's creativity. The structure is as fragile as the tentative new connections that projects such as *Keeping Glasgow in Stitches* and Mixed Threads have made. The fabric of our new multi-cultural society is only pulled together by fine threads that can easily break. It must, as the washing instructions would say, be handled with care. Meanwhile, Mixed Threads continues to make a stronger patchwork from the cultures of different women, stitching them together to bring a new warmth to the city's peoples.

SHIFT AND SPIN
Ewan McVicar

CHORUS
Shift and spin, warp and twine,
Makin' thread coarse and fine,
Dreamin' o' yer valentine,
Workin' in the mill.

Keep yer bobbins runnin' easy,
Show ye're gallus, bright and breezy,
Waitin' till Prince Charmin' sees ye,
Workin' in the mill.

Oil yer runners, mend yer thread,
Do yer best until ye're dead.
Wish ye were a wife instead o'
Workin' in the mill.

Used to dream you'd be the rage,
Smilin' on the fashion page.
Never dreamt you'd be a wage slave
Workin' in the mill.

Used to think that life was kind,
No it isn't – never mind –
Maybe some day love will find you
Workin' in the mill.

He loves you not? So what?
Do the best with what you've got.
Win your pay, spin yer cotton,
Workin' in the mill.

When you choose the thread you need
For crochet or embroidery,
Do you ever think of me?
Workin' in the mill.

Above right
WEDDING SHALWAR
KAMEZ WITH SILVER
EMBROIDERY.
BOUGHT IN
GLASGOW, 1987
Above left PAISLEY
SHAWL, *c.* 1840

FASHION PLATE
SHOWING A SHAWL
DECORATED WITH
LARGE PAISLEY
MOTIFS, 1842

RED KASHMIR
TABLECLOTH WITH
EMBROIDERED
DESIGN

KANTHA
EMBROIDERY, 20TH
CENTURY

MARCH

Joseph Davie studied Fine Art at Glasgow School of Art. He has had several successful exhibitions in Glasgow and London. For this panel he tried to combine the many aspects of the community into a single strong image.

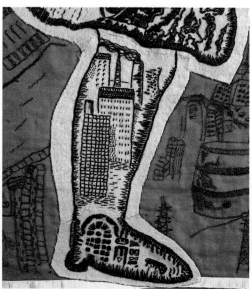

MARCH

The Spirit of the Community

Billy Sloan the journalist was invited to lead a discussion on 'The Spirit of the Community' with adults, children and pensioners in the children's library in Springburn.

"What's special about Springburn?" he asked.

"Fish and chips," said one lad.

"But you can get fish and chips anywhere," Billy said.

"Aye, but no' as good as the ones you get in Springburn."

Nostalgia for a remembered nonpareil of chip shops now gone, led to shared sadness at the loss of industry, loss of local facilities, loss of identity.

"What would you miss if you had to leave?" Billy asked, encouraging introspection.

"Ma bed," came one mournful voice.

"Ma strip."

"Ma dog."

The children reminded us that at the end of the day it is the personal, ordinary treasures that make communities precious.

The recording of the discussion was given to Joseph Davie, the painter and printmaker, as the inspiration for his design. For Billy Sloan and Joseph Davie were both born in Springburn and for the March panel we wanted the spirit of the community to be felt right through the work.

The spirit is personified as half-man, half-woman. Its crown is a factory building, its sleeves are rows of tenements guarded by a pair of Rottweilers. Around its middle are a church and football pitch. The legs are clusters of high-rise flats, cranes, ships and railway engines. The figure juggles with the symbols associated with St Mungo, the tree, the bird, the book, the bell and the fish.

The top of the banner illustrates the various types of housing found in Glasgow. There is a block of multi-storey flats with glazed windows and all manner of curtains. Next, there is the tenement with the occupants trying to outdo each other with the style and opulence of their net curtains and festoon blinds. On the left is a traditional 'but and ben' and on the right, a large villa typical of those built for the newly wealthy industrialists in the 19th century. This particular example bears more than a passing resemblance to one designed by Alexander 'Greek' Thomson.

JOSEPH DAVIE
INSPECTS THE
ENLARGED DESIGN
OF HIS PRINT

The pavement is busy with people of all walks of life going about their business. To the right of the bus which carries the name of The Warehouse, the sponsor for March, there is a lady dressed in purple. This is HM The Queen with the red-haired John Paul Carbery beside her waiting for the No. 51 bus. He is explaining the need for the correct change.

At the top of each banner are the letters spelling out 'GLASGOW 1990'. These are in different metallic textures and because it is difficult to achieve crisp legibility in textiles their construction was complicated. The letters, photocopied on to acetate sheets, were enlarged by means of an overhead projector, then carefully traced on to paper to form the pattern. Cutting and stitching the letters was exacting work and there were some choice words on the day one of the letters was accidentally made in reverse.

At first glance the central image is relatively simple but both figure and background are a complex amalgam of images. The problem was how to translate a powerful yet subtle print image into textile while

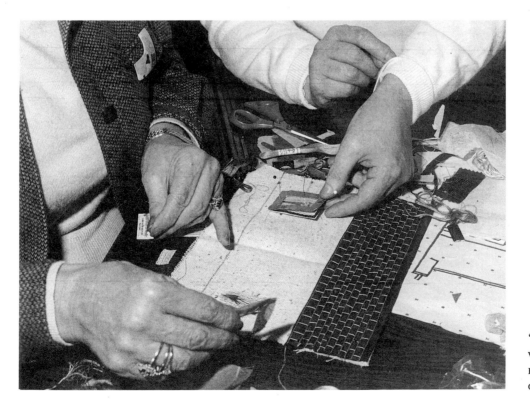

"DO YOU THINK THE WINDOWS SHOULD BE DOUBLE-GLAZED?"

51

retaining the quality of the original? After considerable discussion, stitching and textile printing emerged as the best solutions. Lesley Evans, the workshop leader, began the work in Springburn and took on the task of breaking the design up into 19 manageable pieces, encouraging the workers to interpret the drawing in threads. It was decided to use an old felted blanket for the figure as this would have the visual quality and colour of paper used in Joseph Davie's print. Clare Higney donated one of hers – no sacrifice was too great! The Glasgow Felt Makers' Association had offered its support and this was the ideal design to utilize their skills. Working with children from Springburn's St Aloysius and Albert primaries, Jenny McKay showed them how to card wool and make their own felt fabric embedded with the emblems of Glasgow. Others traced out designs, three children from the ground, two on chairs, with a remarkable show of tolerance of each other's jutting elbows and shadows, as they drew the enlarged projected image.

Another group of children visited the workshops. Being blind they spent a happy hour exploring the January banner with their fingers. They enjoyed the textures and with the aid of descriptions were able to form a mental picture of the banner. We asked what Glasgow meant to them and one replied "Uneven, bumpy pavements". So the pavement

in the March banner is appropriately bumpy.

Once the separate pieces of the body had been embroidered and darned together, work began on the background. Working in monochrome is eye-wearying work, yet with fine thread on yellow chiffon the group achieved amazing intricacy of detail. Only by close inspection will you discover the houses, cranes, pylons, figures, dogs and even newspaper headlines. This was a real labour of love. The Springburn Happy Circle and others in the group are of that breed of women who believe in seeing a job through.

It is true to say that the embroiderers found the discipline of working with a limited palette rather dull, especially after the glitter and vivid colour of the February banner. But when the banner was assembled they discovered that the image, although completely different, had its own vitality, that an equally beautiful effect had been created. The finished embroidery is a faithful interpretation of the original print but with its own integrity created by the individuals stitching, in their own spirited way, the image of their community.

"ARE YOU SURE THERE WAS A HAMPSTER IN HERE?"

MONOLOGUE

I'm Margaret Burniston. I'm 71 years old and I've lived in Springburn all my life like my parents before me. I was born and brought up in Adamswell Street and then went to Balornock in 1928. When I got married in 1948 we couldn't get a house of our own so we stayed with my parents. My three children were born there and two of them are still at home. I suppose because I still have so many things of my grandparents and parents in the house that old Springburn is still very much alive for me. It's full of memories.

If you come to Springburn now you can't even visualise what it used to be like. All the old landmarks are gone, all the old haunts. There is no cinema. The Public Halls, where I heard Harry Lauder in my youth and went to many a dance, is derelict. There's only one school left and the old Springburn that we grew up in, worked in, where we had our families, has gone forever.

Then you couldn't move in Springburn at lunchtime or teatime for the mass of folk coming out of their work. There was pride in Springburn then. We were all respectable working-class folk, a good class of folk. When I think what it was in my days, Springburn was really like a small town. You didn't need to go into the city centre to get anything, you had Hoey's, where you could get anything from a needle to an anchor, and the Co-op. It was a big blow when they closed.

There is a lot missing in Springburn now. Sometimes I wish I'd left, but well, I've always been part of it somehow and I still know lots of people and they know me. We've all known each other since we were wee. It's not just nostalgia and the memories, people are writing books about Springburn now, about the locomotive industry and ordinary life because the history is important, my history, our history.

Part of a monologue performed at the unveiling of the banners,
16 December 1990

Above left MARGARET
AND HER BROTHER
PETER IN THE
GARDEN,
SPRINGBURN, 1928
Above right
MARGARET AND JOHN
BURNISTON'S
WEDDING
PHOTOGRAPH,
19 JUNE 1948

MARGARET AND HER
CHILDREN, 1955

THE SPIRIT OF THE COMMUNITY
Mark O'Neill

This banner is based on the memories of the people of Springburn, a typical Glaswegian community. The peoples of Partick and Pollokshields, Govan and Rutherglen, Townhead and Easterhouse, Drumchapel and Hyndland may find this objectionable – who do the people of Springburn think they are? Glasgow was, and is, a city of villages, each of which has its own fiercely loyal population. The sense of place is very specific; it was these streets, this school, these shops, this park, these baths, these back courts in which they grew up, not in any other, no matter how similar. Thus, the objectors are right to ask "Why Springburn?" But Springburn serves to make the point that the spirit of the community is associated very much with specific places. Springburn represents those places, those villages, which have been destroyed.

For Glaswegians whose childhood neighbourhoods have been destroyed there is a perpetual sense of loss, a dull pain which is only relieved in fond reminiscence. There are many among those who have moved away to the schemes who return regularly, for a drink in a surviving pub, a reunion in a declining church, now dwarfed by high flats. The attachment is not, however, just to the place but to the way of life of the tenement. Technically, this is a building divided into separate houses with a common stairway or 'close'. More picturesquely, it has been described as a vertical village. This is the most common form of dwelling in urban Europe – only the misguided English foster the illusion of living in the country by having houses with back and front doors and gardens.

Until the 1960s, two thirds of the people in Glasgow lived in tenement houses with one or two rooms, single-ends and room-and-kitchens. The most typical arrangement was in four-storey tenements, with two room-and-kitchens and one single-end on each landing, 12 houses in all. These houses did not have bathrooms and the three families shared a single toilet on each landing, as well as a boilerhouse in the back court, each taking it in turn to do their washing.

TENEMENTS IN BAIN
STREET, 1977
(*K. Ingham, Partick
Camera Club*)

The pressures on space, and on people, in such cramped conditions were very great, but they taught people how to live closely together. If privacy was difficult there was also little loneliness. The crowded houses were not suitable for children to play in, but there was little traffic on the streets and the back courts were well within maternal view and shouting distance. At a time when social standing in the community was directly related to age, older people expected to be listened to, so that there was constant supervision by adults of all children in public. Your granny or your aunty lived around the next corner anyway, so you couldn't get away with much. In more ways than one child-rearing was a communal practice.

At a time when most people lived near their work, and work was based on a few large heavy industries which were subject to booms and slumps, people tended to experience unemployment together. Poverty was a collective as well as an individual and family experience. Before the Welfare State, people had to make their own provision for economic disasters, and those who could afford to were members of friendly societies which provided basic sickness and funeral insurance. Trades unions, co-operative societies, churches and a whole range of

MR J. THOMAS,
SENIOR, BY THE
GLEAMING RANGE IN
HIS LIVING-ROOM,
GOURLEY STREET,
SPRINGBURN, 1940S
(*John Thomas, Junior,
Springburn Museum Trust*)

recreational clubs all provided other forms of mutual support and help. The absence of free health care also meant that people lived their entire lives at home. Women gave birth at home, in conditions which led to a very high death rate among both mothers and babies. The bodies of the dead, young and old, were laid out in the room. And death came earlier than elsewhere. Glasgow was the TB capital of the world until the eradication campaign of the 1950s and many factories had dangerous and unhealthy working conditions. Life held many more life-and-death experiences than now, and much of the richness people miss is tinged with tragedy.

The poverty during slumps and the minimal standards of living

MR & MRS WILSON IN
THEIR LIVING-ROOM,
8 BAIN STREET,
CALTON, 1977
(*Malcolm R. Hill*)

during periods of employment meant that pleasures were enjoyed to the full when they were available. Celebrations such as New Year family gatherings and weddings were savoured, as were dancing and the flickering dreamland of the cinema.

The communal way of life based on work, home and mutual support in the face of harsh living conditions has been undermined by the changes of the past 40 years. The severe problems of overcrowding and poor public health were tackled by the wholesale destruction of tenement neighbourhoods. They were replaced by building types unsuited to communal living – tower-blocks, flat-roofed deck access blocks whose layout encouraged vandalism. The sense of place was also undermined by the scale of the demolition and the mass movement of people to new towns and housing schemes on the outskirts of the city. Even the Welfare State, in the process of creating better conditions than ever before in history, undermined the voluntary organisations by making them redundant.

For many people, then, the sense of community is not rose-tinted nostalgia but a memory of something which was real. No one denies the hardship, nor the consequences for individuals and families who slipped through the fragile safety nets of the informal and voluntary support groups. These problems were real – all too real. But for many, this community spirit is more than a memory, it is an ideal. It aspires to mutual interdependence, combining individual self-respect with support in a way which is made very difficult by modern patterns of living and working. It is an ideal people know can be achieved because they have experienced it. The banners of *Keeping Glasgow in Stitches*, in the way they were designed and made, show that it is still possible to organise at least part of our lives in this co-operative way. The apparently nostalgic Spirit of the Community banner is as much about the future as about the past.

COWLAIRS CO-OP,
MILLBANK STREET,
SPRINGBURN, *c.* 1932
(*Springburn Museum
Trust*)

60

Right PLAYHUT AND
CHILDREN, 1976
(*J. G. Gillies, Partick
Camera Club*)

AN EVENING CHAT:
TENEMENT LIFE IN
THE HOT SUMMER OF
1976
(*Malcolm R. Hill, Partick
Camera Club*)

DEMOLITION,
GALLOWGATE, 1970S
(*K. Ingham*)

APRIL

Lindi Richardson studied Embroidery and Woven Textiles at Glasgow School of Art and the Royal College of Art. In her design she tried to bring out the use people make of the parks and to include some of the interesting features in them.

APRIL

Dear Green Place

April's banner is a celebration of spring in the city. The colour has warmed up considerably and the parks and gardens are bursting into life. The term 'Dear Green Place' comes from a translation of the ancient Celtic name Glascu and the words can be found glimmering in the river.

The richly detailed inner banner was designed by Lindi Richardson whose own work always shows her gentle sense of humour and acute observation of people and their quirks. The design brief suggested that the image should show people enjoying Glasgow's many parks and open spaces and Lindi produced a design which amalgamates some of the best features of several Glasgow parks. Our springtime stroll begins at the top left where we find the Art Gallery and Museum in Kelvingrove Park. Appliquéd birds are busily nesting in exotic trees created in silks and satins, ruched into shape and held in place with stitchery. The cherry trees on the right are confected from soft pink yarns worked in large French and bullion knots.

We arrive next at The Queen's Park pond full of ducks and with the magnificent Stewart Memorial fountain nearby. To the left is a busy play park with all the usual play equipment which has been created in wool-wrapped wire and pipe cleaners by the children of the Young Embroiderers' Society.

All the figures have been created in stumpwork, taught in a special workshop by Doreen West, Chairwoman of the Scottish Embroiderers' Guild. This padding technique was popular in the 17th century for decorating domestic objects and we chose it because The Burrell Collection has a particularly interesting group of original 17th-century stumpwork pieces and we wanted to champion its existence with a modern version in *Keeping Glasgow in Stitches*.

The lamp-post, complete with Glasgow's coat of arms, now stands outside the People's Palace on Glasgow Green. This one was made in exquisitely fine handmade lace by Jean Leader of the Glasgow Lace Group.

Next we encounter the Kibble Palace glasshouse, created by couching fine cords – to represent the glazing bars – over a background of gauze fabric to suggest the glass and the plants inside. There is also a prize-winning display of tulips and daffodils and even a bed laid out to form the symbol of Road Safety Week.

A favourite pastime of Glaswegians, whenever the sun shines, is to line the park benches. Two elderly ladies are taking the opportunity to catch up on gossip and to enjoy the activity of joggers, baby-walkers and numerous dogs at play. Honey, the beagle on the right, is a particular favourite, smooth, sleek and lightly padded.

Finally there are the magnificent Queen's Park gates worked in black cord with gilt areas of padded gold kid. The stone gate posts are fascinating, with their carved swags of flowers created in textiles.

Sitting just outside the gates is Baajie, Malcolm Lochhead's beautiful ginger cat. Malcolm was concerned by the number of dogs in

DESIGN FOR DOGS
AND BEDDING
PLANTS

the banner so his cat was included to redress the balance. Baajie's facial expression suggests he is deciding which dog to 'see off' first. Hanging on the park railings is a little board emblazoned with the logo of Benson Design, Glasgow, the sponsors for April.

The inner banner is contained within a handsome and colourful framework with the letter S set against a rising sun. The strong light throws into silhouette one of the finials designed by Charles Rennie Mackintosh for the east gable of the Glasgow School of Art. The original is constructed from wrought iron but interpreted here in black silk rouleau. The sun is made of a subtle combination of tulles, chiffons and metallic fabrics and threads. The inner disc suggests the changing seasons.

There is an interesting proportional relationship between the inner and outer banners. At the beginning Malcolm decided that the banners should be tall and slim, but exactly how tall and what size the inner image should be was another matter. He stumbled upon some esoteric research conducted in the late 19th century which showed the preferred

Left MARY STIRLING MAKES THE QUEEN'S PARK GATES
Right THE STEWART MEMORIAL FOUNTAIN

THE QUEEN'S PARK
GATES COMPLETED

ratios between the sides of rectangles as selected by men and women. After furious calculations – no mean feat for a non-mathematician – he arrived at an outer banner measurement of 15 feet by 4 feet 6 inches and an inner banner measurement of 7 feet by 4 feet. This proved fortuitous, as many fabrics are between 48 and 54 inches wide. Even more fortuitous was the discovery that the pillars of the central hall of the Art Gallery and Museum are of the same proportion. Perhaps Sir William Simpson, the architect of the building, had consulted the same research. The inner banners were then positioned at varying heights in order that those with greater detail would be lower and therefore easier to see, while those with strong graphic content would be higher and more striking.

'April is the cruellest month. . .' wrote T. S. Eliot and for the organisers of *Keeping Glasgow in Stitches* this proved to be the case. With February and March banners being completed, April on the go, designs for May and June underway, commissions for October and December being negotiated, this was the month of looking back, forward and straight ahead all at once. We were saved by the Embroiderers' Guild who took full responsibility for the creation of the April banner under the diplomatic leadership of Pat Brown.

With eight branches of the Guild poised for action and knowing that skilled embroiderers like challenges we decided to forego the general principle of collective decision-making and instead gave each branch one landmark, one person and one dog to do in the techniques of their choice. Eight sets of photographs by David Peace, photographer at Summerlee Heritage Museum, and eight tracings were made and each set was given a name. Each branch then drew a name from a hat. It was a good plan, but there was a bit of post-draw bartering as swops were made in private deals between branches. At first the sections were worked in the branch's own areas, while representatives worked on the background fabric at NeedleWorks' base in preparation for the appliqué of all the images.

What a feast for the public April proved to be. There were so many techniques to witness, from needleweaving to quilting, felt sculpture to goldwork. The sight of the experienced confidently at work equipped with the tools of their trade – sewing kits, needlecases and necklaces of magnifying lenses – was a real treat.

Left BAAJIE, THE GINGER CAT
Right CARVED SWAGS ON THE PILLARS OF THE QUEEN'S PARK GATES (*David Peace*)

MESSING ABOUT ON
THE RIVER

LINDI RICHARDSON
SHOWS SUE
HUTCHESON OF
BENSON DESIGN THE
WORK IN PROGRESS

GLASGOW'S PARKS
Walter Gilmour

The parks have always been very dear to the hearts of Glaswegians. They bring a sense of freshness and beauty to the city. Glasgow parks are unique, not because there are more open spaces devoted to parks and recreational facilities per head of the population than any other European city, but because they have so much history within them. They are a permanent tribute to the energy and ability of the civic authorities in the 19th century.

Once you start looking at the history of each park and the monuments within it you begin to unfold a fascinating picture of the life of the city itself. There is the historic Green, jealously guarded by the East Enders, scene of everything from political demonstrations to pop concerts; Queen's Park, the site of the Battle of Langside and named for Mary Queen of Scots; Kelvingrove Park, where major international exhibitions were held in 1888 and 1901 and where the city fathers spent £10,000 to build the granite stair near Park Gardens in 1854; and the McLellan Arch, now near the Courts, which has been moved so often it's a wonder it's not travel sick! These historic events are only one aspect of the picture because Glasgow parks are rich in personal histories. Everyone has strong memories of their own local park and of more adventurous family outings or Sunday School picnics to distant unfamiliar parks.

There are fascinating people associated with Glasgow's horticultural history too, many of them unknown. How many people have heard of Peter Barr, 'The Daffodil King'? He was born near Copland Road in 1826, the son of a Govan weaver. Although he began life as a weaver's draw-boy, his main interest was flowers. In those days Govan had fields of cowslips! Soon he was running the seed department of James Thyne in the Argyle Arcade and eventually established his own company in Covent Garden, London, which is still going strong under the name of Jaegar. His main interest was in daffodils and soon a display of some of the many fine species he introduced into cultivation will be established in the walled garden in Bellahouston Park.

We are fortunate that early on it was recognised that the open spaces were the one great deterrent to the physical deterioration of the people at a time of increasing industrialisation, when the city was growing rapidly and these open spaces were under pressure from the builders. We can enjoy them just as we can enjoy the magnificent trees which are a legacy from the old private estates. However, there are some legacies we can do without, like the old batteries – we used to call them accumulators – which continue to be dug up in Bellahouston Park dating from the time the army was billeted there in the 1940s.

Of course, there have been changes over the years. There are fashions in horticulture just as there are in everything else. Today, the new parks are of a recreational nature and don't have an ornamental priority, but there is probably a better balance of use. Things are much more relaxed today: have you noticed that there are no longer any 'KEEP OFF THE GRASS' signs? This wasn't always the case. Some of the city's benefactors laid down very strict rules on the use of parks. For example, Mrs Elder, whose gift benefited Govan, stipulated that:

KELVINGROVE PARK AMID PREPARATIONS FOR THE 1901 INTERNATIONAL EXHIBITION. IT WAS ACQUIRED IN 1852 AND LANDSCAPED TO THE DESIGN OF SIR JOSEPH PAXTON
(*Collection: Walter Gilmour*)

No person shall exercise, or break in a horse, ass or mule.
No cattle, sheep, pigs or goats are allowed to pass through the
Park.
No person shall wash any clothes in the lake in the Park, nor
place or dry clothes in the Park, or on the railings . . .
beat, shake, clean carpets, mats or rugs in the Park . . .
No person shall wade, bathe or fish in the lake . . .
No person shall discharge any firearm, or set off any balloon
or fire balloon . . .
No person shall sing, read or recite any profane or obscene
ballad . . .
No person shall expose wounds or deformities . . . inducing
the giving of alms.

THE STEWART
MEMORIAL FOUNTAIN
ERECTED IN 1874
COMMEMORATES
LORD PROVOST
STEWART, TO WHOSE
ENERGIES THE CITY
OWES ITS
MAGNIFICENT WATER
SUPPLY,
INAUGURATED IN
1859

Certainly the biggest change has been caused by the Clean Air Act which has totally changed the plantings in the parks. Shrubs that only just survived in the past now grow to double the height and even the grass thrives. The lime or linden trees planted because they tolerated the awful air pollution are now flourishing – indeed pilots flying into the airport call Glasgow the Linden City because of the colour of the lime trees, especially in autumn. Some recent research has calculated that every lime tree supports 300,000 aphids. This astonishing fact will come as no surprise to car owners who park underneath them!

Cleaner air is obviously of great benefit, but there have been a few unforeseen problems. Glasgow sparrows may have lost their coughs but the roses now have Black Spot which was never seen before.

There are some changes for the worse, especially the loss of the 'parkie'. He was a familiar figure doing the rounds, picking up rubbish with his pointed stick as he went. Usually a local chap who knew all the regulars, he could cause instant fear or panic with one blast from his whistle. At the end of the day he would walk round the park ringing his bell before locking the gates.

Probably my favourite park, now largely destroyed, was Rosshall. With its artificial rock dell, secret pool and island with a weeping beech, it was a wee gem. The artificial stone was made of pulhamite, invented by James Pulham in the early 19th century. Now there was a fascinating and ingenious character. He created an improved form of Portland cement which was used for all sorts of garden ornaments and simulated stone still to be found in many famous gardens such as St James's Park and Buckingham Palace.

The thing about Glasgow's parks is that there is something for everyone: from Ruchhill and Queen's Parks' tremendous views over the city and beyond; Tollcross's International Rose Trial Beds; the Botanic's Orchid collection; and bedding plants in Victoria Park and George Square; to Pollok's demonstration garden (one of the first to be established) and, of course, the picturesque Highland cattle. This award-winning fold of about 70 animals has a long association with Pollok. Although they look so ferocious with those awesome horns they have a placid nature. The calves, which look just like teddy bears, are a delight.

Did you know that we even have our own ghosts? These have been seen in the part of Queen's Park known as the Deil's Kirkyard, which was the burial site of some of the troops after the battle of 1568.

I wouldn't be at all surprised if there weren't a few of those parkies around too!

It always amuses me to think that the parks have people from the cradle to the grave. We are taken to the parks as babies in our prams; we feed the ducks and swans, or play on the swings as children; we stroll with our first love, oblivious to all around us; in middle age we jog to fight the flab and in our old age, sitting on a bench, we watch the cycle repeat itself. At the end of the day the Parks Department is still there running the cemeteries and crematoria. But this isn't a gloomy thought. Our parks are a wonderful legacy for the future, we should enjoy and cherish them. They are unique.

In conversation with Liz Arthur

THE KIBBLE PALACE, ORIGINALLY A CONSERVATORY ON THE ESTATE OF THE ENGINEER JOHN KIBBLE AT COULPORT, LOCH LONG. IT WAS MOVED TO THE ROYAL BOTANIC GARDENS AT HIS EXPENSE AND OPENED IN 1873 *(Collection: Walter Gilmour)*

AT FIRST THE KIBBLE
PALACE WAS USED
FOR CONCERTS AND
MEETINGS BUT IN
1881 IT WAS
PLANTED OUT WITH A
FINE COLLECTION OF
TREE FERNS
(Collection: Walter
Gilmour)

THE QUEEN'S PARK
MODEL YACHTING
POND EARLIER THIS
CENTURY
(Collection: Walter
Gilmour)

THE QUEEN'S PARK
POND IN WINTER
(*Collection: Walter
Gilmour*)

A FAMILY OUTING IN
SPRINGBURN PARK,
1950s
(*Springburn Museum
Trust*)

YOUNG LOVE, 1991

A PLAYPARK, 1991

HIGHLAND COWS
AND CALVES, POLLOK
PARK

JOGGERS IN POLLOK
PARK, JUNE 1991

MAY

Andrew Hay is an entirely self-taught artist who formerly worked as a lorry driver and shop steward. His aim for the May banner was to create a bold but simple design in the tradition of political banners.

MAY

Paint the Town Red

One of the first themes to be decided was that May should be concerned with Glasgow's socialist history; that it should celebrate people, not politicians. Nevertheless, when Norman Buchan MP died later in the year we dedicated the banner to him in memory of his untiring work on behalf of the arts in Britain. The other positive decision was that May should be red. This works well within the overall colour scheme, allowing July to be bright and the winter to be represented by the cold colours of the spectrum.

Some experts were consulted about which key images should be included. Janey and Norman Buchan, Euro MP and MP respectively, Bob Brown, former News Editor of the *Glasgow Herald* and Elspeth King and Michael Donnelly of the People's Palace Museum, advised the artist Andrew Hay. He approached the design of the inner banner from his standpoint as a painter. He took a 7 by 4-foot canvas and created his design in oil paints, but he had an additional problem as the high position of the inner banner dictated that the letter G would occur within the image. He produced a bold and very red painting.

The theme is also a celebration of banners. There is the raising of the Red Flag in George Square in 1919 and a crowd of figures united around a banner celebrating the centenary of May Day. This is worked in traditional goldwork techniques where jap gold thread is couched on to the red satin background to form the letters. At the right, to symbolise decline, two figures are folding away the banner of Upper Clyde Shipbuilders which closed in 1972, while in the foreground four young people are unfurling a new one based on Cranhill Arts' poster design for May Day 1990. It was painted using fabric colours and then cleverly worked so that the images can be seen on its outer folds.

Although at first the members of the group were decidedly uneasy about the theme, they were reassured that *Keeping Glasgow in Stitches* was a project about our city and all its aspects – to avoid Glasgow's

Right ANDREW HAY
PUTS THE FINISHING
TOUCHES TO HIS
DESIGN

Left STUDENTS FROM
JORDANHILL
COLLEGE CREATE A
CROWD

political past would, indeed, be dishonest. Rising to the challenge they set to work armed with lots of reference books. Lech Walesa slipped in, so too did a banner for Ravenscraig Steel Works, threatened with closure.

Students from Jordanhill College created some of the figures of the crowd using a clever and novel technique developed by NeedleWorks. Surprisingly enough, the images were actually photocopied on to fine fabrics, creating the impression of a sea of flat cloth caps to represent the scale and strength of feeling of ordinary people on that day. The larger figures are worked in layers of felt and calico to create a bas relief effect, the small figures are worked in monochrome wool flannel and tweed, with details of the faces and garments provided by simple stitchery.

The banner includes two references to the work of Glasgow sculptor George Wyllie – the paper boat, symbol of Glasgow and the Clyde's lost shipbuilding industry, which was lowered into the river in 1989, and the straw locomotive, representing Springburn's lost railways. The locomotive hung from the Finnieston crane during Mayfest

1987 and was ceremonially burnt. For this reason you will find a slightly ghostly steam engine and tender set against a background of glowing embers at the foot of the banner and, at the top, the crane and paper boat. You will also notice that the river has taken on a distinctively red cast to represent the Clyde. Women from the Auchentoshan Adult Training Centre worked very patiently to produce the red stitchery. The gold fabric of the letter G is shot with red to accentuate the overall theme.

The remainder of the outer banner is filled with 12 red and gold framed photographs. Andrew Hay suggested that it would be appropriate to photograph a group of visitors to the museum to represent the people of today and to 'freeze' a moment in the making of the banner. So on a Saturday afternoon in mid-May Derek Copland photographed a representative selection of visitors. You will find among their number a pair of twins, a father and daughter, a mother and son and even a small boy with a black eye!

Andrew Hay stayed with us throughout the workshops, helping with the fabric painting, advising on tone and encouraging the work with compliments and genuine admiration for the way his painting was brought to life. Visitors stopped uncertainly by the bold banner. "This," said one of the original hesitant members of the group, betraying a note of pride, "is the raising of the Red Flag in 1919 in George Square. One of the great moments of Glasgow's Labour history when if Britain was to have a revolution it would have happened here . . ." We like to think the project had its own small revolutions.

DOROTHY ALLAN
PUTTING A DISSIDENT
IN HIS PLACE

RAISING THE RED
FLAG

MARGARET LEGGAT
HAS IT TAPED

GLASGOW'S LABOUR HISTORY
Liz Carnegie

The year 1888 saw the opening of the magnificently palatial Victorian City Chambers – symbol of Glasgow's municipal pride – in George Square. The same year saw the formation of the Scottish Labour Party – led by Keir Hardie. Thirty-one years later, the two came together on 'Bloody Friday' (31 January 1919) during the Forty-Hour Strike when the Red Flag was raised over George Square.

The Forty-Hour Strike of January/February 1919 was so called because its main objective was to reduce the working week to 40 hours and thereby improve working conditions and reduce the inevitable post-war unemployment. On 'Bloody Friday' thousands of strikers had assembled in George Square to hear the Lord Provost's response to a

SCOTTISH LABOUR
PARTY MEMBERSHIP
CARD, 1893

request that he should intervene with the Government on their behalf. Police were sent in, a riot ensued and, in the days that followed, troops occupied George Square. Although some concessions were subsequently gained with regard to working conditions, the strikers did not win their 40 hour week.

The crucial event of the Great War for many Glaswegians had been the Russian Revolution of 1917 and the Government feared its influence – hence the heavy-handed reaction to the Forty-Hour Strike. To the post-war Coalition Government, the strike seemed to confirm the threat of a Red Revolution in a Glasgow already known as 'Red Clydeside' largely due to the influence of figures such as James Maxton, leader of the Independent Labour Party (which absorbed the Scottish Labour Party), and John MacLean, who in 1918 was appointed Soviet Russian Consul in Glasgow by Lenin.

However, Labour history is about people and not personalities and is expressed not just in the high points which can distort experience but is also reflected in the daily lives of all. From the Calton weavers' strike of 1787 to the Upper Clyde Shipbuilders work-in of 1971 (and

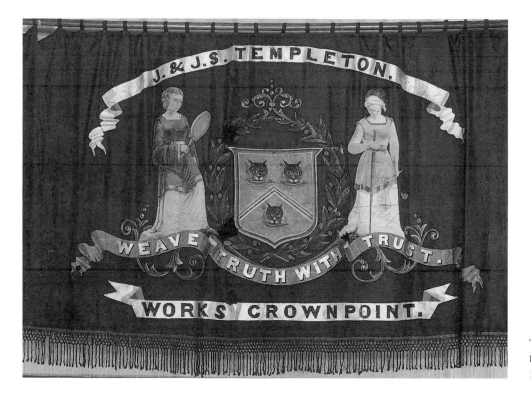

TRADE UNION
BANNER, TEMPLETON,
19TH CENTURY

RENT STRIKE, THE
DEMONSTRATION IN
PARTICK, 1915

RAISING THE RED
FLAG, GEORGE
SQUARE, 1919
(*Glasgow Herald*)

beyond), industrial conflict in Glasgow was the inevitable consequence of a clash of interests between organised labour and national (and, increasingly, multi-national) capital.

Glasgow's rise to prominence as an industrial capital was largely due to its large potential workforce, copious raw materials and – in the case of its 'keynote' industry, shipbuilding – a sympathetic natural habitat. There was a time when shipbuilding became almost synonymous with the Clyde and the expression 'Clyde Built' was an internationally recognised guarantee of quality. At the industry's peak immediately before the First World War, there were as many as 42 yards on the river. Similarly, Springburn became a world leader in locomotive manufacture and between textiles and tobacco – not to mention the ancillary industries which fed the shipyards – Glasgow could rightly claim to be the workshop of the world.

The tendency for employers to treat labour as an exploitable natural resource has ensured that, from the early combinations and friendly societies through to organised trade unions, the workers' aims have always remained the same: to secure as a right a recognised

MAY DAY, LONDON
ROAD, 1930S

90

standard of working and living conditions for all. In 1911, against the background of massive industrial development and organised unrest leading to national strikes by dockers, seamen and railway workers, a crucial strike developed out of a lock-out at the Singer's Sewing-machine Factory in Clydebank (started by the women in the needle-making department over piece-work rates) and, after an increasingly bitter struggle, the management succeeded in breaking the strike and dismissing all of the activists involved, although many of them went on to become shop stewards on Clydeside during the 1914–18 War.

The Clyde Shop Stewards' Movement (which developed out of an engineers' strike in 1915) formed the Clyde Workers' Committee which actively fought against 'dilution' – the employment of unskilled and semi-skilled men and women on skilled work. Its newspaper *The Worker* was suppressed by the government for its opposition to the war. John MacLean had also preached against the war (declaring that what was wanted was a war against capitalists and not a capitalists' war) and, in the following year, both he and Maxton were jailed for sedition. MacLean's early death at the age of 44 resulted from his long spells in prison and official harassment outside it – and this made him a significant socialist martyr.

Although all the great (or remembered) public figures of 'Red Clydeside' were male and the heavy industries remained the exclusive preserve of men until the necessities of the Second World War, women figured prominently in the Temperance and Peace movements as well as that of women's suffrage (which the pressures of the war brought to a conclusion with the granting of the vote to women over 30 in 1918). It is important to realise that not all the struggles of socialism were industrial for this would deny the vital contribution of women in history. Women such as Agnes Dollan were the dominant force in the 1915 Glasgow rent strikes in protest against massive increases in rent for houses built as stabling. After all the groundwork done by the 250,000 tenants on rent strike, the protest reached its climax with sympathetic industrial action by the engineers and shipyard workers which forced the National Coalition Government of the time to concede a Rent Restriction Act, returning rents to their pre-war levels. Such concessions tend to be hard won and short lived, however, and 1920 saw another rent strike, this time Scotland-wide.

In 1921 the onset of mass unemployment and the three-month lock-out of British miners resulted in another infamous Friday in the calendar of Scottish Labour history – the 'Black Friday' of 15 April 1921 – marking the collapse of the seemingly powerful Triple Alliance of miners, railwaymen and road transport workers. The head of revolutionary steam which had been built up in Glasgow finally seemed to evaporate and the subsequent wage cuts which were enforced across many industries put the cap on it. The TUC deliberately kept Glasgow's major industries of shipbuilding and engineering out of the 1926 General Strike until the last moment and the Depression conditions of the '30s, the creeping de-industrialisation which followed the Second World War and the galloping de-industrialisation of the last decades gave Glasgow precious little foothold on fraternal achievement. The famous UCS (Upper Clyde Shipbuilders) 'Work-In' of 1971 was successful at first in staving off the Government-imposed closure of the shipyards but the action was ultimately futile in the face of the eventual dissolution of UCS at a time when there was a worldwide contraction of shipbuilding and the onset of a Government which was set on ridding itself of responsibility for state-maintained shipbuilding at any cost and which did not believe in anyone's 'right to work'.

The question why (as asked by George Wyllie) industry was allowed to die is too emotive, too uneasily felt to be easily answered here but the *Straw Locomotive* (1987) – hung from the Finnieston Crane before being ceremoniously burnt at Springburn – is not just a requiem for the people's past but is a celebration of that past and therefore offers symbolic rebirth – or, in the case of the paper boat (1989), relaunch. Similarly, the Cranhill Art Centre's projects use art as a continuum: to record the past and show the present is to create a context for the future. There were Red Flags flying over George Square in 1919, flags and banners raised on every May Day (the international workers' holiday since its conception in 1889), banners used to protest and celebrate or unify and to create an atmosphere of carnival – and banners for 1990.

Glasgow's industrial past was not killed by culture but culture must not be allowed to deny or obscure that past.

ANTI POLL TAX
DEMONSTRATION,
1989

DEMONSTRATION IN
SUPPORT OF UPPER
CLYDE
SHIPBUILDERS, 1972

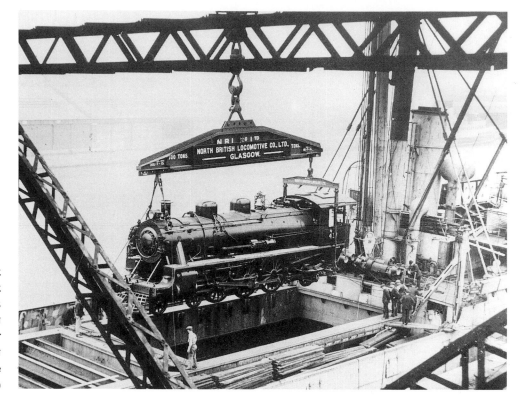

A RAILWAY ENGINE
FROM THE
SPRINGBURN WORKS
BEING LOADED ON
BOARD SHIP AT
FINNIESTON
(*Springburn Museum
Trust*)

GEORGE WYLLIE'S
STRAW LOCOMOTIVE,
1987 (*George Oliver*)

NORMAN BUCHAN MP
Selected by Janey Buchan MEP

Norman Buchan, the much loved MP for Paisley South, died in October 1990. The many tributes to him have spoken of his qualities as a teacher, radical politician, peace campaigner, indefatigable supporter of the arts, but above all of his generosity of spirit and his warmth and sincerity as a gentle, humorous man.

Through his deep love of the written and spoken word he was intensely interested in folk music and was always writing poems, songs and satirical parodies. Danger at work was a constant interest and he wrote 'The Auchengeich Disaster' at the time of the underground fire in the pit near Chryston on 18 September 1959.

THE AUCHENGEICH DISASTER

In Auchengeich there stands a pit,
The wheel above, it isna turnin'.
For on a grey September morn
The flames o' Hell below were burnin'.

Though in below the coal lay rich
It's richer noo, for aw that burnin'
For forty seven brave men are deid,
Tae wives an' sweetherts ne'er returnin'.

The seams are thick in Auchengeich,
The coal below is black an' glistening
But och, its cost is faur ower dear
For human lives there is nae reckoning.

Oh, coal is black an' coal is red,
An' coal is rich beyond a treasure;
It's black wi' work an' red wi' blood –
Its richness noo in lives we measure.

Oh, better though we'd never wrocht,
A thousand years o' work an' grievin'.
The coal is black like the mournin' shroud
The women left behind are weaving.

Sung to the tune of an old folk song
'Skippin' Barfit Through the Heather'

'Last Night' was written by a Canadian, Ed McCurdy, a song which regularly had verses added to suit the campaigns of the time. Norman Buchan wrote this verse at the time of the Polaris campaign. His wife Janey Buchan said: "We were all very affected by the very closeness of Glasgow to the base and by the awfulness of it being in such a beautiful part of the country." It was sung at his memorial concert on 26 January 1991, in the Concert Hall, Glasgow.

Last night I had the strangest dream
I ever dreamed before
I dreamed I saw the Holy Loch
In flames from shore to shore
I dreamed I saw the mountain tops
The rivers run blood red
And all around sweet Mary's Loch
The silence of the dead.

Mary's Loch was the old name for Holy Loch

JUNE

The design evolved from two workshops, one group of women led by writer Liz Lochhead, the other by artist Sam Ainslie.

JUNE

A Woman's Life

On a Saturday morning in May, Liz Lochhead arrived breathless at the creative writing workshop organised as the first step to the June design. The small mixed group of women aged from 20 to 80 listened attentively as she read her poetry, laughing sometimes at the neat truisms of the words. Liz set them to work, coaxing from them stories and experiences, childhood memories and adult pain. By the end of the day each had something to work on and all knew a little more about each other. The following Saturday Glasgow artist Sam Ainslie met with another group of women. With the words of the first group and extracts from 7.84's *Govan Stories*, a locally written and professionally performed hit of the 1990 Mayfest, they developed the themes, the myths and realities of a woman's life. By the end of the day there were sheaves of paper, lots of phrases, descriptions to use as inspiration in the finished work and a hastily drawn Shiva with each of her multiple arms clutching an object of necessity in the different roles and aspirations of women.

Lorraine Davin and Sandi Kiehlmann led the workshops with humour and ingenuity. We were after something lively, not a moan, but a banner that made spirited points with warmth and self-knowledge. Workshops became discussions about what should be included. What should the hands hold? What should the framed images being juggled include? What should the apron pockets contain? Eventually the resplendent figure emerged. There are exquisite cameos depicting the seven ages of women, there are the tools symbolising the roles each woman assumes. Two hands hold open a book containing the demands of the women's liberation movement. Her lowest arm cradles a baby. There was some dissent among the participants as to how the baby should be dressed. Eventually a peach cotton dress was specially crocheted for the perfect Glasgow wean. The woman's hair is tangled with some of the sayings from the writers' workshop and she wears an

97

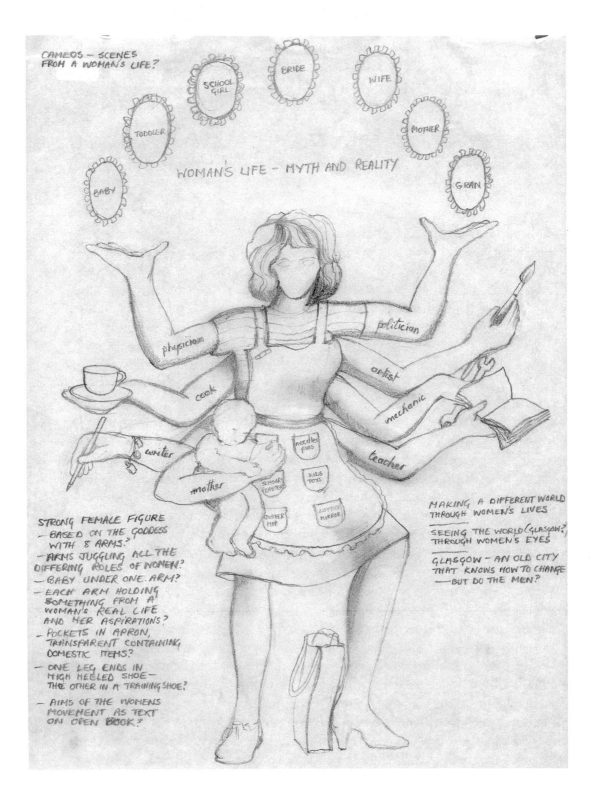

THE ROUGH OUTLINE FOR THE BANNER

apron with a red cross denoting her role as a nurse and pockets filled with the trappings of domesticity. Her legs are different, one realistically varicose veined, the other vampishly glamorous.

Throughout the background are words and phrases which make telling reading – heartache, headache, backache and colloquial Glasgow phrases such as 'hamell dae me'. Brave to the last, women's rights are listed, the contraceptive safely tucked in the apron pocket and emblazoned in bright yellow is the rallying cry 'Jobs for the Girls'.

The border was a free for all, with everyone sewing in haberdashery: zips; suspenders; hooks and eyes; safety pins; old buttons. In fact, all the things one would find tangled in a button box or sewing-machine drawer.

The upper image is punctuated by a washing line which symbolises the perceived domestic role of women. The participants rose to the challenge of making miniature garments to hang on the line. Among them is a white sweatshirt carrying the logo of the June sponsors, BP Exploration. Next there is a remarkable pair of blue knitted socks measuring just 2½ inches, complete with turned heels – a difficult enough procedure working full-scale, but these were made using four cocktail sticks. All the garments are held in place with genuine miniature clothes pegs.

The regiment of women represents several different types. There are two little girls dressed in the very correct clothing of the 1950s, and Richard Keir's teddy bear dangling from the hand of the gingham-clad girl was an agreed triumph, even if it was made by a man. There is the ragged barefoot waif from the backlands of early 20th-century Glasgow and the suffragette proclaiming the demand for universal suffrage for women. Finally, there is the woman of the '90s complete with her small son. The detail is so minute that the child's blue top is even decorated with a tiny Thomas the Tank Engine.

In the centre of the large letter O is another small banner proclaiming the philosophy suggested by Shirley Conran's motto that 'Life is too short to stuff a mushroom'. The June banner was shown to Dr Macief Ramus of the Polish Ministry of Culture, who was curious to know the meaning of this statement. On hearing the explanation she said that she would dearly love a similar project to take place in Poland but there were two problems: a) that only a relatively wealthy country could afford to do it; and b) that Polish women were too busy stuffing mushrooms!

DOROTHY ALLAN,
NAN BYRON, SHEILA
PATON AND
MARGARET
MCLELLAN AGREE
THAT THIS BEATS
HOUSEWORK

Above them all, sailing serenely down the Clyde, is a ghostly PS *Jeanie Deans* – ghostly because, like her sister paddle-steamers, she no longer plies up and down the Clyde, but one of the older participants told us a classic story of the *Jeanie Deans*. Apparently a little girl had been put on board by her grannie at the Broomielaw. The grandmother asked one of the other passengers to tell the child when they arrived at Dunoon. The passenger forgot and when he remembered rushed to the captain to explain the predicament. The captain turned the ship around and returned to port. "This is Dunoon," said the hapless passenger. "Oh good," replied the girl, "I can eat my sandwiches now."

"I THINK I'D RATHER
BE STUFFING
MUSHROOMS"

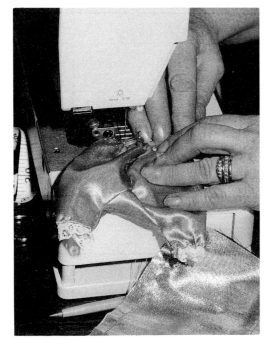

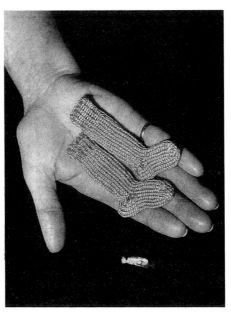

Left DOUBLE
GUSSETS
Right A LABOUR OF
LOVE

"ARE YOU SURE THERE'S AN O IN 'WUMMAN'?" NANCY BAILLIE-SCOTT

Left DETAIL
Right BAREFOOT WAIF

A CLASSIC EXAMPLE
Libbie McArthur and Eirene Houston

(Two 'Glesga wifies' sit smoking, drinking 'callies' and gabbing)

Rena: Lizzy, would you say you were a classic example of the stereotypical image of the Glasgow working-class wifie, as a down-trodden, ill-educated, indeed oppressed victim of a deeply entrenched, decadent, distempered, capitalist system?

Lizzie: [Long pause] Uch aye.

Rena: Me tae! And would you say that this role that you find yourself cast in, actually effectively lends into the hands of your oppressors?

Lizzie: [Long pause] Uch aye.

Rena: Me tae! Aye, I cannae help feeling I started to become the woman I am today at a very early age.

Lizzie: *My* ma smoked 60 Capstan Full Strength a day all through her pregnancies.

Rena: Did that no' leave her a bit short?

Lizzie: Aye, but you didn't notice, she got a pair a high heels free with all the coupons.

Rena: Aye, I cannae help thinking our mothers' expectations of us were, well, less than inspiring.

Lizzie: When I was a wee lassie I says to my ma – I says – "Ma" – I says – "what will I be when a grow up?" She looks at me and says . . . "A wummin, whit dae ye think, stupid."

Rena: Well . . . I expect she didnae want tae see you disappointed.

Lizzie: Talking about being disappointed, my pools coupon never came up again.

Rena: Lizzie, hen, I'm right disappointed in you, does it no ever occur to you that the temptation of an instantaneous profusion of material wealth is the very carrot dangled in front of our eyes by oor oppressors in an effort to divert our energies away from the real issues – there is no such thing as an easy answer to the poverty trap we find ourselves in. [Pause] Mine's never came up either.

Lizzie: Never mind, hen, I thought your Janice was going to be a rich and famous snooker player?

Rena: Aye, that's oor Janice.

Lizzie: Aye, well, she's got the balls for it.

Rena: Aye, an' I'm getting her the cue next Christmas.

Lizzie: Let's face it, in these times of chronic industrial decay nae wonder the weans dream about being celebrities. They might as well, there isnae any real jobs.

Rena: Oh aye. And what's a 'real job'? What you're doing there, by using the word 'real' in the context of 'real job', is you're presupposing a uniform reality which we all wish to embrace.

Lizzie: So! [Pause] I wouldnae mind embracing a wee bit of uniformed reality myself right now.

Rena: Listen you, this could be a time for us to explore, redefine and develop our spiritual and creative urges.

Lizzie: Her at number eight was going on about her primal urges the other day in the queue at Henry Healys.

Rena: Oh aye, what like?

Lizzie: Well, I couldn't help feeling her urge to go to the Amazonian jungle to uncover her roots was denying the essence of her current reality. I telt her she'd be better nipping next door to Luigi's and getting him to cover her roots.

Rena: Here wait a minute, I think I feel a wee primal urge coming over me right now.

Lizzie: No, hen, that's just the Carlsberg, it does that when you warm it up at the fire.

Rena: Oh.

Lizzie: Are you for another?

Rena: Uch, aye.

Lizzie: Me tae.

Performed as Lib 'n' Rene

MAITLAND STREET,
COWCADDENS, JUNE
1911

BY THE CATHEDRAL,
c. 1910 (*Glasgow
Herald*)

ANNA MUNRO OF DUNFERMLINE, ORGANISER OF THE WOMAN'S FREEDOM LEAGUE,
GORDON STREET, GLASGOW

LEAVING

It's all arranged. The bags are packed and waiting to be loaded in the car parked at the back out of sight of the neighbours. There'll be Grace next door sat on the bedroom window-sill watching everything that's happening. I hope Joan, two doors away, doesn't pop in with her gay smile and non-ending chatter. My stomach's churning, I'm beginning to sweat. I can feel the blood pounding through my veins.

Bubbles, don't sit there watching me with your tail between your legs. Those eyes. You know, don't you? Do you know? I'm sure he does.

I'm glad Carly and Anthony are playing safely in the garden at Helen's.

I must hurry. I start loading the black bin bags and cases in the car, Bubbles watching me and following my every trip. The car seems so far away, though it's only about 20 yards.

Look back to the house. It looks so welcoming but look again. Up the stairs, the dark stairs. Round the corner to the bedroom. Cold place! These walls with the pretty flowered paper. My head pressed against it. That big strong hand holding my throat tight, tighter. The other curls into a fist. Again, again, again! Pretty pink paper spattered with blood. Will it never end, carrying these bags. My whole body shakes. The final slam of the car boot.

Go on, Bubbles, you can't come, go back to Our John, he'll look after you. Goodbye John, tell Mum not to worry, I'll get in touch soon. My eyes are filling with tears as I start the engine. Have I got everything, it's too late now. I turn the car into the cobbled street, the row of terraced houses with their windows like eyes watching me as I drive slowly off.

From the Writing Workshop

MEN
Liz Lochhead

Men see men I've had it
Up to here absolutely
It's all off completely.
I said suppose that'll suit you fine I said
You can go out with your mates
Every night of the week and not just Thursdays
I said,
Look at the state of you
The beer's all going to your belly already
And coming from the West of Scotland you
Are statistically unlikely even to reach the age of 25
without false teeth
And to tell the truth
Since we got engaged
You never bother with the Brut
or the good suit I said,
I'm sick to the back teeth of
Every time we go for a Chinese
You order
chicken and chips, fried egg and peas.
I said No way
Believe me the only way I'd ever consider
The World Cup in Mala-bloody-ga
For my honeymoon
Is if I was guaranteed
An instant trade you in for a
Six foot shit-hot sharp shooter that never failed to hit the spot.
I told him where to stick his bloody
One carrot diamond-is-forever.

I blame his mother.

SCOTTISH WOMEN'S
MARCH TO LONDON
AGAINST THE SLAVE
BILL, 1930S

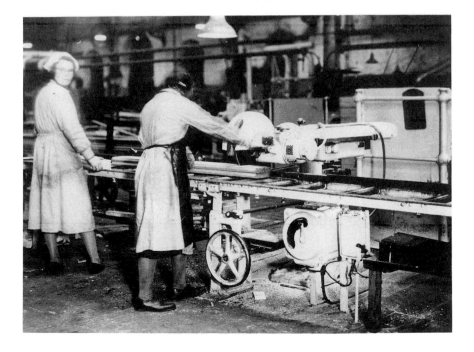

WAR WORK: WOMEN
IN THE COWLAIRS
RAILWAY WORKS,
SPRINGBURN
(*Springburn Museum
Trust*)

HANK WINDING, TEMPLETON'S CARPET FACTORY, 1976 (*J. G. Gillies*)

Right
WASHING, THE HARD
WAY, 1955

WASHING, THE EASY
WAY, 1/6d (12½p)
FOR 8 LBS, 1955

Left SPRINGBURN
MUMS, 1991
(Susan Scott)
Right JOYCE DEANS,
BEARSDEN, ELECTED
AS THE FIRST WOMAN
PRESIDENT OF THE
ROYAL
INCORPORATION OF
ARCHITECTS IN
SCOTLAND, MAY
1991 *(Granville Fox)*

JULY

Teacher and artist Brian McGeoch organised design workshops for 30 children who experimented with torn paper, fabric and simple collage to create their design.

JULY

The Glasgow Fair

July was traditionally the month when Glaswegians had their holidays and traditionally went 'Doon the Watter for the Fair'. Until recently the seaside resorts were reached by paddle-steamer. Alas, only one remains, the PS *Waverley*. She has become a powerful symbol of holiday-making on the Clyde.

For the banner, photographs and postcards of the ship were closely examined by the participants who were determined that the details should be accurate. As a result we have a near perfect textile model complete with tiny holiday-makers sailing in a rippling river of haphazardly cross-tucked striped silk.

The banner has two distinct sides. This came about for two reasons. The first was that this is the turning point of the overall colour system when the colour begins to cool in August. The other is that the weather for the Fair is notoriously unpredictable and so the left side shows the Fair in the rain. Here the family are fighting valiantly with their umbrellas in a summer downpour which is probably just a passing shower as there is a rainbow, beautifully executed in chain stitch.

Behind the letter W is a large summer sun partially obliterated by rain clouds. It is overlaid with running stitches in silk to give the effect of a heat haze. Basking in its relentless heat is a slightly overweight Glaswegian on the sands of the Costa Packet. He has turned a fetching lobster pink and his string vest (hanging on the sun umbrella) has left a vivid line on his chest. He has, however, taken some precautions against sunstroke. He is wearing a handkerchief knotted at the corners as an attractive sun hat. Ironically, the Glasgow Fair in 1990 was glorious with record-breaking temperatures.

Another feature of the holiday is that a fair is traditionally held on Glasgow Green, hence the glittering coconut shy. The silhouetted figures are competing for prizes of Teenage Mutant Hero Turtles which were all the rage with children that summer.

PS *WAVERLEY* The inner banner was designed and worked by children. For three Mondays in June, Brian McGeoch of the Museums' Education Service, with Amanda Thompson from NeedleWorks, organised design workshops with 30 primary- and secondary-school children. One of the schools in Canniesburn became so enthusiastic that the staff and pupils organised their own *Glimpses of Glasgow* project with NeedleWorks hosting sewing workshops for children and their families at the school. The design workshop introduced the children to shape, colour, composition and texture by guiding them through experiments with torn papers, fabric pieces and simple effects of collage. Then, in July, the stitching began. As with the adults, we wanted them to discover new ways of doing things and responded to an offer made by the West of Scotland Guild of Weavers, Spinners and Dyers by inviting them to work with the children. The children learned how to make their own fabric, to spin and to weave, and Jean Leader, of the Glasgow Lace Group, held lacemaking lessons and was unfailingly good humoured and patient with her young pupils.

The banner was sponsored by Liberty's, who also provided all the fabrics, and the adults had to suppress their anguish and their envy as

Left INTERPRETATION
OF THE DESIGN
Right CREATING THE
SUN WORSHIPPER

40 children uninhibitedly tore into shot silks and printed lawns that their elders would have killed for. When Liberty opened a new shop in Buchanan Street a group of children was invited to work in residence for the day. There they sat among luxurious fabrics and soft furnishings sewing their Mutant Hero Turtles. Such a scene would have been unimaginable when *Keeping Glasgow in Stitches* was first thought of, but it was just one of the many surprises the project held in store.

Although the workshops were aimed at the eight to 14-year-olds, younger brothers and sisters slipped in, no one having the heart to send them away, so the youngest participant was actually four years old. In a riot of activity, lace cranes, the 'Barras', a mouth-watering knicker-bocker glory and truly magnificent, succulent fish and chips, complete with pickled onion, were produced. Children playing on a farm, holiday-makers sailing and swimming and a Punch and Judy show in full swing demonstrate the children's embryonic talent and inventive use of newly-learned skills and techniques which had emerged under the guidance of Bell Caven and Stacia Rice. They achieved a glorious result.

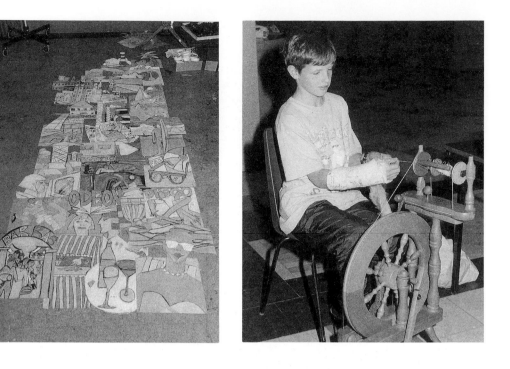

Left THE CHILDREN'S
DESIGNS
Right "I NEVER KNEW
SPINNING WAS SUCH
A DANGEROUS
OCCUPATION!"

"I'LL NEVER GET A
MATCH FOR THIS
COLOUR"

"I'D LOVE A LIBERTY
... BODICE?"
WORKSHOP IN THE
BUCHANAN STREET
SHOP

LEARNING TO MAKE
LACE

THE GLASGOW FAIR
Liz Carnegie

July – the Fair fortnight, and it's 'A Rerr Terr Arra Ferr' or 'Doon the Watter' on the *Waverley* to Rothesay (and will it rain?) or a flight to Spain for two weeks of summer sun.

The Fair, established by the Charter of King William the Lion, *c.* 1190 – to be held in mid-July between the Feasts of St Peter and St Paul – is 800 years later remembered more as a time than an event. The Fair itself has changed in emphasis over the years to reflect the nature of employment and people's expectations, to become a time for carnival and children's events. In pre-industrial times (and before 1820 when it was moved to the Saltmarket) its chief purpose was to trade livestock, but this was always a time for celebration and holiday-making. Entertainment was provided by shows, circuses and menageries, which travelled to Glasgow and offered the chance to marvel at the unknown, rare and strange – such as the birth of twin lion cubs in Wombwell's Menagerie in the 1820s or, on a darker note, the many freak-shows which drew the crowds with voyeuristic intent.

Soon, thanks to the advent of the steamboat in 1814, people were leaving Glasgow during the Fair for the resorts 'doon the watter' at Rothesay on the Isle of Bute or Dunoon or Largs or even Ireland, as fleets of ships left the Broomielaw for a whole new holiday experience. There is some irony in the fact that the industrialisation which made this possible also brought about the pollution which made an annual leave of absence desirable. Cycling clubs and rambling clubs (popularised by Hugh MacDonald's *Rambles Around Glasgow* – published in 1854) also aimed to spend leisure hours where the air was fresh. Indeed, Fresh-Air Fortnights were organised by charitable and evangelical groups for people who would not otherwise have a holiday and, by 1870 (when the Fair was at Vinegarhill and therefore out of the city centre), going 'doon the watter' was so established that only the very poorest would spend the entire fortnight in Glasgow. This remained the holiday-making pattern until the '50s when, just as the world had been opened up by the steam-boat, cheap air fares to Spain for the Costas served to shrink it and offered the option of package holidays to lands traded with but until then unseen.

AT THE BROOMIELAW, GLASGOW. 5256 GWW.

PADDLE STEAMER AT
THE BROOMIELAW

ON THE BEACH AT
HELENSBURGH,
EARLY 1900S

ON THE BEACH AT
SALTCOATS, EARLY
1900S

MEMORIES OF THE FAIR
Mrs J. Dreghorn

'Glasgow Fair.' Folks say it and smile. There's a gladness in the air although the rain's stottin' down.

My memories are of going away – all the family – there were eight of us – sometimes doon the watter and sometimes to the Fife coast as my father was a Fifer. What a performance that was! The hamper was brought out the week before from under the kitchen bed and packed with all the bed linen and clothes. It went two or three days before us, 'Collected Conveyed and Delivered', for about 2/6d. Of course, you had to have railway tickets. Our cat, Topsy, whenever she saw the hamper appear sat on top of it till it was collected. She knew she was going to be left with the neighbours. We kids with all our decent clothes packed went about in our old duds and winter shoes as the sandshoes were in the hamper. In our day you all went off on holiday dressed in your Sunday best – complete with gloves. I remember one year the train we got on was so dirty that my mother put down newspapers for us to sit on to keep our white frilly knickers clean!

In our day there always seemed to be plenty of trains and steamers around and the authorities always prided themselves that everybody who was going away got away. They just kept putting on extra trains.

All the big works closed down on Fair Thursday for ten days' holiday. The pubs did good business then with the men having their holiday pay and there were plenty of 'merry' men floating about giving wee boys pennies and saying, "It's the Ferr".

Some stay-at-homes used to go up to the top of Cathkin Braes on Fair Sunday just to see over Glasgow without its smoke pall. Quite a sight, the works being shut down.

The shows were there at Glasgow Green. All the fun of the Fair. If we had a lot of rain the grass disappeared into mud but we squelched about and enjoyed it.

Shettleston and Tollcross Community Centre AIR Group

ON THE BEACH AT
SALTCOATS, EARLY
1900s

MAY BOWIE, 1932

FROM THE FAMILY
ALBUM

SUMMER HOLIDAY
Scott Rybarczyk, age 9

One summer morning I woke with excitement. I was going to Blackpool. When we got on the bus I said to myself This is it! I love it! We finally got there. Wow! Blackpool Tower is really big. "It sure is," said my Gran. The last night we were there we went to the fun fair. It was Super Duper Great. There was a ghost train and everything you could imagine. The worst day was when we had to go home.

THE END

Kelvinhaugh Primary School

MY HOLIDAY
Karen-Louise Neary, age 10

When I was five I went to Ibiza, that's an island near Spain. The worst part of the holiday was the packing, oh you should have seen it! There were clothes everywhere and all you could hear was Mum shouting, "Don't do this, don't do that, you can't take this, no not that!" – well when that was over I thanked my lucky stars there was no more shouting just peace and quiet. Of course, I went to bed early as we had a busy day ahead of us.

The next day I got up at five-thirty (well, we can't all stay in bed like some people reading this can) and got dressed. Mum and Dad were already up, so I had my breakfast, got washed, hair combed and shoes on. As soon as we were ready Dad phoned a cab and it came in under five minutes (you may be wondering how I knew that so I just wanted to tell you I could tell the time). When we got there, Glasgow Airport was packed with people. When we got on the plane I had to suck a sweet or my ears would pop. After the sweet was finished I fell asleep.

When I woke the next morning I was in a hotel room, I think it was number 237 I'm not sure, anyway when I woke, Mum and Dad were on the veranda eating breakfast. Mum told me to wash my face and give her and Dad a hug. I did both, of course. When we had finished breakfast we got dressed and off to the beach.

On the beach I went for a swim, well not exactly more like a doggy paddle. After that I did try to swim but it didn't work so I asked Mum to sit on a rock and me hold on to her legs but what Mum didn't know was that there was a huge insect on her bottom! When she and I were finished my little swim she got up and was ready to go away when some girls screamed and I laughed and one ran away. Mum didn't know what was the matter until I told her, then can you guess what she did, she screamed! Luckily for her she didn't fall off.

Mum soon recovered and the next day we went down to the same beach and sat on the same rock. I had my swim and when I finished Mum asked me to buy her ice-cream so I got up on the rock and went down a path to the shore, got my Dad and got ice-cream. When we came back the tide had come in, Mum was sleeping as well as stranded! We soon got her off that rock but with great difficulty.

After two weeks we had to go home and on the plane we watched a fat lady singing opera. We were soon home and I was glad to see Margaret and Michael and Judy and I was glad to sleep in my own bed.

St Marnock's School

HOLIDAYS
Michael Garrity, age 10

I was so excited, I just couldn't wait, I was going on my holidays to Girvan with my friend Brendan who just stays round the corner from me. But the one thing I hate about holidays is packing. My mum is so worried in case I forgot anything and by jings I didn't, how could I? The day before we went I helped to tidy up (unlike me), I have never done so much work in my life except in school!

Well, soon the big day arrived and before I knew it I was away. It took one and a half hours to get there and it was horrible passing by all the farmers' fields, what a reek! I thought that was bad well, I was in for a surprise, I didn't know we were going to pass a sewage works! Soon we arrived at the little house (it was my aunt's), quite a nice little one painted red. The street was called 'Cauldshore' and they were right! But we did get some good weather. Brendan and I played at tournaments on a stretch of grass which was half a mile long. On the second day we went to the Amusements and I nearly lost all my money but I won some back. We went swimming every day and I learned to swim but at the end of the holiday we were like prunes! One day we went to Stranraer. It was a nice run and you could see Ireland. When we reached Stranraer we were starving but all the shops were closed!

On the second day my mum and big sister went back home, but we stayed on. A couple of days later we went to phone her. We got a Chinese, me and Brendan got a chicken and cashew nuts while my dad and my sister got a beef curry. One day my dad came out to play football and I didn't realise he was that good, unfortunately I had to be dumped with my big sister while Brendan got my dad. We got beaten 11–10!

The beach was all done up, it was nice. We went on the paddle-boats and the shows were there. The bouncy castle was enormous and there was no doubt I was going on it. I thought I was going to bong right out of it! We got a game of putting and a game of crazy golf. I won (hurray!). The journey back was as bad as the journey up! It was stinking and worst of all my dad's cousin stayed across the road from the house and she had two daughters! I hated them and I was squashed in the car. I had two drinks and a chocolate bar and I felt sick – no wonder with the smell outside! When I arrived home my big sister was so happy to see me and funnily enough I was happy to see her.

St Marnock's School

AUGUST

Lex McFadyen studied Fine Art at Glasgow School of Art and now works as a fashion designer. In the August panel he tried to pick out the essence of Glasgow Style through tongue-in-cheek stereotypes.

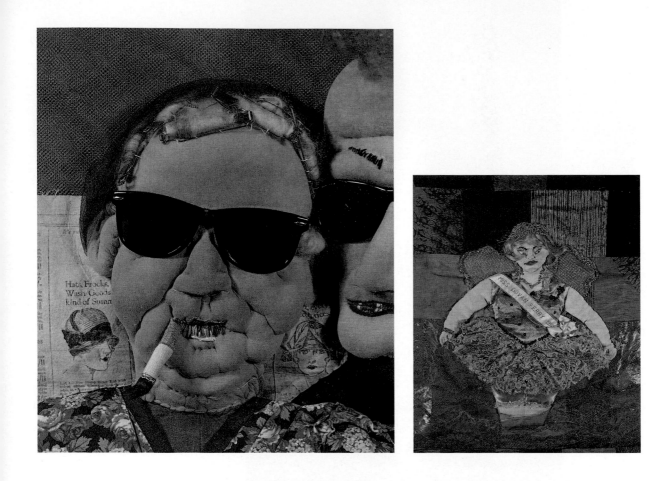

AUGUST

Glasgow Style

In August we encounter a rather fortunate gap. The 11 digits of 'GLASGOW 1990' meant that August would not contain either a letter or a number. By then we had been through a range of atmospheres. There had been the restraint of January; the chatter and bustle of February; serious dedication for March; skill and experience in April; commitment and care in May; laughter and ingenuity for June; an exhaustingly active July and then August – the month of the grotesque and genuine Glasgow.

The banner is full of irreverent references. Until comparatively recently, small passenger-ferries plied backwards and forwards across the Clyde. The Govan ferry has become part of the folklore of the city, personified as the 'Govan Fairy' in Christmas pantomimes, so there she stands in August, the Govan Fairy, up to her knees in the River Clyde, resplendent in her best green and magenta gown showing more than a glimpse of her pink satin knickers.

The anonymous queue of 'types', all wearing trendy Rayban sunglasses, was designed by Lex McFadyen and assembled piecemeal, limb by lifesize limb, under the guidance of Lynn Mack. The grotesque pile of stockinette-covered, carved-foam fingers, feet, ears, arms and torsos grew alarmingly, and visitors to the Museum were taken aback by a sewing project that displayed such signs of ghoulish good humour as the painting of the finger nails of a hand not yet attached to its owner. How far from meticulous cross-stitch could you get?

At the head of the bus queue we encounter a Glasgow grannie-figure who became affectionately known as Aggie. She is a force to be reckoned with as she stands, arms akimbo, with a cigarette clasped tightly in her pursed lips. We can deduce that she has only left home briefly as she still wears her slippers, but there is a clue to where she has been as her discarded, unsuccessful bingo card lies on the pavement.

Immediately behind her is a tough, muscle-bound young man

sporting a tattoo on his arm. He is fashionably 'cool', dressed all in black with enormous black leather 'docs'. Next in line is a rather snooty Kelvinside lady who is obviously going out to lunch with the girls as she is wearing her best suit. But she is not all she seems, as she is stealthily lifting a £5 note from the young man's pocket. Then there is a slick spiv-type, followed by the hip-hop fan with his skateboard and very expensive trainers. Finally Senga (a genuine Glasgow name), who definitely enjoys a good time but is not a good-time girl and whom a later male participant swears he used to date. Best described as a fashion victim, her hair has suffered just too many blond rinses and she perhaps has had one sun bed too many. However, she wears the badges of her fashion, her gold chains, with pride, and the ubiquitous white high heels will soon trip the light fantastic round her handbag at the local disco – that is, if she can gather up the contents of her over-stuffed handbag before the bus arrives, including a *Daily Record* newspaper representing the August sponsor, the Scottish Daily Record and Sunday Mail (1986) Ltd.

If you examine this banner with care you will discover some gleeful details that really bring home the spirit of the project: the cigarette stub on the sole of the trainer; the Bluebell matchbox clutched by Aggie and the pickled onion lying among the remains of a discarded

130

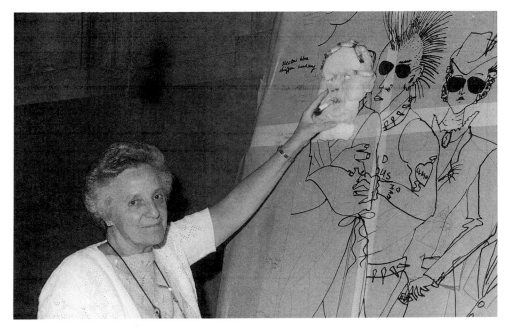

KATIE DURIE CHECKS
AGGIE FOR SIZE

fish supper. There are many other details. A plea in local newspapers for old and new clothing labels from Glasgow shops brought an enthusiastic response. These have been sewn together into ribbons which are threaded through the piece to symbolise the fact that our 'types' are both bound together and being tripped up by style.

On a more serious note there are oblique references to the other Glasgow style, created by Charles Rennie Mackintosh and his contemporaries in the late 19th and early 20th centuries. The words 'The Glasgow Style' are worked in gold leather in lettering originally designed by Mackintosh. The rose, affectionately known as the Glasgow Rose, is a popular motif seen on many buildings, furniture and decorative works. It is a recurrent theme in the work of Jessie Newbery and Ann Macbeth who established Glasgow as an internationally renowned centre for the teaching and development of embroidery. To honour this heritage a miniature banner with a rose worked in the traditional materials of linen and floss-silk thread was embroidered by the niece of one of the Glasgow Girls whose work was being exhibited and celebrated in an exhibition at the Art Gallery and Museum at the same time.

Watching people go round the banners you see them come to August and laugh. There is an immediate chuckle of recognition at characters that you've known and met at one time or another. The group tackled an ambitious idea with verve and, although it seemed grotesque in the making, the finished work is a true caricature in textiles, using the printed cotton of a real wrap-over apron and the stretch fabric of Senga's skinny-rib to take the caricature closer to life than would have been possible in any other medium.

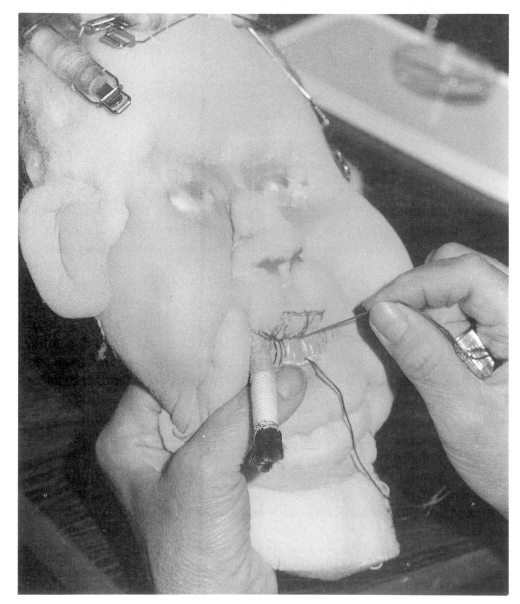

LIP SERVICE

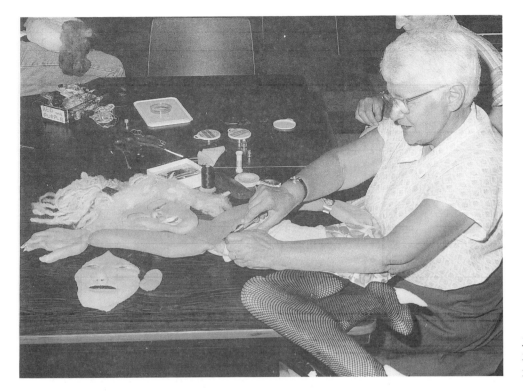

JEAN MORRISON
MAKES A NEW OUTFIT
FOR SENGA

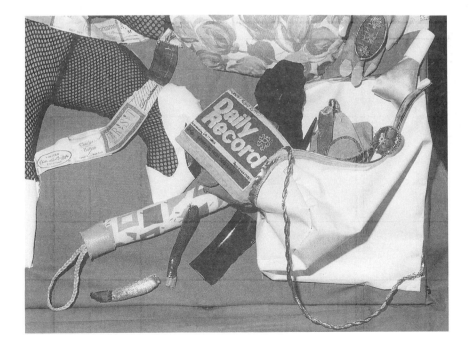

THE CONTENTS OF
SENGA'S HANDBAG

WHAT IS GLASGOW STYLE?
Liz Arthur

Glasgow is not a city that is regarded as a great innovator of fashion. Rather, it follows the main trends but with its own inimitable stamp which has more to do with attitude than details of style.

Here you will find every conceivable style from quirky retro dressing in second-hand clothes to the restrained, discreet elegance of beautifully-cut classics. Here the conservatively dressed rub shoulders with the outrageous and the downright shabby. But there is a great Glasgow tradition that says, 'if you've got it, flaunt it' and some who 'flaunt it' even if they've never had it in the first place.

One of the first street styles taken to the hearts of working-class Glaswegians was that of the 1950s' Teddy Boy. Inspired by Edwardian tailoring with details borrowed from the American urban jazz culture

FUSCO'S BARBERS SHOP, CAMBRIDGE STREET, JUNE 1955. SPECIALISING IN CREW AND TONY CURTIS CUTS, IT WAS POPULAR WITH TEDDY BOYS

— zoot suit — and influenced by rock 'n' roll and Westerns, it was a distinctive, extravagant fashion. Young men with velvet-lapelled drape jackets, drainpipe trousers, crepe-soled brothel creeper shoes, bootlace ties and fluorescent pink, orange or lime green socks, decorated street corners menacingly. And in every dance-hall these aficionados combed their carefully cultivated Tony Curtis quiffs. How many of them still hanker after this swaggering style and keep that suit at the back of the wardrobe, just in case? This symbol of defiance, once the uniform of local gangs and condemned by the Establishment, is now no more than a nostalgic memento of lost youth.

The Teds gave way to the more upmarket, sharp-suited, pointed-toed Italianate style of the Mods. An occasional middle-aged female Mod, caught in some strange time-warp, can still be seen in mini skirt, beehive hairdo, thick mascara and pale lips. Clicking her way along the pavement in white high heels she attracts wry, condescending smiles from the fashion cognoscenti; but she's gallus and doesn't care. She knows she looks great.

Left TEDS, 1950S
Right HOSPITAL PORTER BY DAY, GUN SLINGER BY NIGHT AT THE GRAND OLE OPREY COUNTRY MUSIC CLUB

The Punks, on the other hand, provoked more aggressive or more wary reactions. Yet this ugly, subversive, rebellious style was energetic and creative, using ordinary, everyday things to shock. For example, the young man seen in Argyle Street carrying a kettle as a handbag and with a biscuit on a string threaded through the safety pin in his ear was being completely original. How totally different is the style of the smart, besuited business men and women with their individuality hidden behind a neutral uniform, or the sporty-type, clad in expensive trainers and designer track-suit. What does it matter if the image is not true, as long as you look the part?

There is nothing especially distinctive about this mix of styles — these figures are seen in every British city. The wee woman in headscarf, curlers and square coat, carrying a shopping bag, is surely a universal figure recognised everywhere from the Gallowgate to Gdansk. It is not the style that is different but the Glaswegian attitude to it.

(Willie Gall cartoons first published in the Glasgow *Evening Times*)

"Ah don't think ah'd suit that colour, Agnes!"

"It's easy ... jist tuck yer frock intae the bottom o' yer knickers."

Left PUNKS AND
SKINHEAD, 1985
(*Glasgow Herald*)

URCHIN STYLE BY
DEBB AT VIDAL
SASSOON, PRINCES
SQUARE
(*Neil Mackenzie Smith*)

After London, people in Glasgow spend more on clothes than anywhere else in Britain. But even London doesn't have the number of top designer clothes shops concentrated into such a small area. Menswear in particular is more adventurous in Glasgow than elsewhere. Young people with money who rush to London in search of the trendiest clothes are amazed when they realise there is nothing in London that they cannot buy in Glasgow. It is no accident that Katherine Hamnett and Emporio Armani chose Glasgow as the site of their second British outlets. Yet despite its new image and abundance of shops, Glasgow still has its problems of deprivation and unemployment, but these, far from discouraging an interest in stylish dressing, may indeed be the reasons why it flourishes.

Glasgow style goes back a long way. In the old close-knit communities it was a matter of pride to look presentable and to take care of one's appearance, even in the most difficult circumstances. It may be an old cliché that the Sunday-best suit pawned to help feed the family during the week had to be redeemed in readiness for the weekend, but it was a fact. This was not high fashion, more a consideration of appearance and maintaining an image, of defying deprivation. It was a way of uplifting the spirit. If you look good, you feel good.

Perhaps for the same reason hairdressing became important. One of the most dramatic ways to change your appearance is to change your hairstyle, and Glaswegians were adventurous, demanding high standards to which local hairdressers responded, winning international renown in the process. Irvine and Rita Rusk, Taylor and Anne Ferguson are among the city's best, and hairdressers now come from all over Britain to attend their seminars. It is yet more evidence of Glasgow's sense of style.

Style is also about the Glaswegians' love of having a good time, of dressing up to go to the dancing; of Saturday nights when sisters vied with each other for the best clothes and when the first out of the house was the best dressed. The arguments and recriminations would be faced on Sunday, but it was Saturday night that mattered. The music of Joe Loss and the big bands may have given way to Glasgow groups such as Wet Wet Wet, Hue and Cry, Blue Nile, Deacon Blue and Simple Minds, and the dance halls may have been replaced by clubs and discos, but stylish dressing is still every bit as important. The Lycra-clad customers queue outside the trendiest clubs and only those appropriately dressed gain admission.

Until the 1950s there was no such thing as teenage fashion, but today stylish dressing starts at a worryingly young age, and there is a strata of fashion-conscious schoolchildren, too young to attend the clubs. Some congregate in Central Station and are identifiable by their conformity to the group image, but within that group image there are subtle differences unnoticed by the uninitiated. These youngsters, too young to have developed a strong personal style, avidly follow magazines such as *The Face* and *Blitz*, the arbiters of style. Many of them finance their embryonic fashion consciousness from paper rounds and

139

Saturday work, using their earnings to buy expensive clothes that take weeks to pay off.

Yet interest in fashion is not confined to the young. It is spread across the whole age range – witness the number of glamorous grannies around – and attempts have been made to harness the fashion consciousness of the city, using the abilities of young graduates from the School of Art and Cardonald College to create the basis of a new industry. Milan has a major design industry which regularly lures our best designers to Italy but there are many who question why we cannot utilize their talent locally. Despite the hype surrounding the Glasgow Style promotion of 1987 when the District Council, Scottish Development Agency and the Third Eye Centre joined forces to promote a major fashion event in Amsterdam, that year's European City of Culture, signs of a regenerated fashion industry have failed to materialize. Basically, the problem is a lack of the sort of supporting infrastruc-

A SATURDAY NIGHT IN SPRINGBURN, 1976 (*J. G. Gillies*)

ture which exists for the Scottish pop music industry but which has been lost to the fashion world with the decline of the textile industry in this country. Although there are well-established, successful fashion designers working in the city, the outstanding talents of Helensburgh-born, top couture designer Alistair Blair and the innovative Pam Hogg have needed the wider opportunities afforded by London and Paris. The influential fashion journalists and buyers simply will not travel north and it is easier for designers to work at the hub of things.

Yet the resilient, gutsy swagger of Glasgow's style continues. It may be impossible to define precisely, it may have nothing to do with particular fashions or age groups, but what is certain is that it has everything to do with the spirit of the people and a determination to enjoy life.

TRENDY TEENAGERS
AT A DISCO
(*Susan Scott, Springburn
Museum Trust*)

GLASGOW STYLE
Marcella Evaristi

1

I remember going to Francie and Josie
               when I was wee
My mamma kept patting the back
               of her brand new bubble cut
And telling me to take off my white mohair bolero
               with the pearl buttons
Because I'd be too hot.
I stared at my new black patent shoes and said
               I would not.
Then the lights went up and there
               was this pair
Of hilarious spivs with a sticky-up curl
               like a hook
In one of them's hair, and these short jacket
               suits
With painful tight pants and their ties
Were like liquorice sticks made of lurex
               under the lamps.

(It crossed my mind that look
Was maybe called The Italian Style –
But never asked.
In case she got cross-ish
Capisc'? We were cut from that cloth
               ourselves
Ish.)

Anyway
This wean I was once was killing herself –
They looked so ludicrous!

But they thought their gear
Was gallus,
Was God's gift in stitches –

142

And the laugh   looking back
They were right.

2

Personally, I miss the old department-stores:
Daly's (first and fairest), Copland's, Trérons –
You just won't get the likes of them again.

Dear departed Daly's, you
Who handed me that treasured brooch
The one with the amethyst
                                        nestling so snuggly,
In the silver talons of that big bird's
                                                claw –

Setting off
(like nothing will again)
My French paisley-pattern foulard-style
                                        silk scarf.

When I recently lost that gem
In the so-called Sauchiehall St Centre
(Enough said)
I knew we were talking Dark Ages
I knew the Last Link was dead.
Look at your blank young faces!
You should see your features!

For Daly's was pulled down
Long before you donned your terries,
Never mind your dungarees!
(Terries, dear? They're *nappies*)

So, to fill you in, the place was
Perfumed,
Glamorous,
But not, you know,
Ridiculous.

A smaller Harrods but better, my gosh,
Far fewer tourists
Plus Rennie Mackintosh.

Classy
Not Armani,
More Aquascutum.

A shame they took that tea-room
And my past
And put the boot in.

3

My dad sends me up about my trainers
Son, can't ye tuck yon flappy bits in?
But they're great. God, they cost me

a fortune

An you want to see the look of *him*
Ageing hippy. Wrong denims. Wrong

moustache
(A'd rather die than borrow a Dad-bought shirt)
I caught him once trying on my Raybans.
I laughed. I could see he was hurt.

But still I feel jackpot selfish
With Mum trying to juggle the bills.
Plus I've nothing left over for Christmas.
See my trainers?
They make me feel ill.

Cos what's style when the world's

short of money?
I was dead sure I'd think of that more –
But then Trish said my gear drove her crazy –
See my trainers? *Ten feet aff the floor.*

SEPTEMBER

Malcolm McCormick is a regular cartoonist for the *Daily Record* and *Sunday Mail*, *Daily Express* and *Evening Times*. For September he wanted to include all the Glasgow teams and to convey the lively attitude of the fans.

SEPTEMBER
Football Crazy

A community project should, by definition, involve everyone in the community. *Keeping Glasgow in Stitches* by its very nature appealed more to the women of the city, so we decided to include one banner to be worked by men – if not voluntarily, then at least with gentle encouragement. What better subject to appeal to them than football, Glasgow's sporting passion.

First there is the immaculately tended football pitch which would surely be the pride of any groundsman. Its perfectly straight stripes are achieved with velvet ribbon on a matching felt background, bringing new meaning to the description 'velvet lawns'. Adjacent to the pitch are two groups of people, a triumph of textile skill, using layered coloured nets to achieve solid silhouettes. On the right, the winning team supporters are jubilant, while on the left the losers are skulking home arguing and apportioning blame. One of the participants reminded us of a survey conducted by the BBC in the 1960s to find out the scale of domestic violence after unsuccessful football matches. The interviewer asked a Glasgow woman, "Is wife-beating common when a supporter's team loses?" She replied, "Oh aye, awfy common."

The background colour of this banner could not be either green or blue, the colours of Celtic and Rangers, and so the compromise colour of turquoise, a mixture of the two, was chosen. It was equally important not to offend the supporters of the other teams in the city and so an integrated supporters' group of the five leading clubs was created. Malcolm McCormick, the well-known cartoonist, was responsible for designing the inner banner. He works in black and white so his design has a strong graphic quality which has been enriched with the clubs' colours. He had never been involved with textile work before and was fascinated by the possibilities of the medium.

The design begins with the names of each teams' stars being chanted by the supporters. Then high above the stand is a confusion of

bunnets and scarves thrown in the air by happy supporters. There is
the red and white of Clyde; black and white of Queen's Park, the
longest established club in Scotland; white and blue of Rangers; red,
black and yellow of Partick Thistle; and finally the green and white of
Celtic.

The stand is crowded with over one hundred supporters. They
were traced on to white cotton from the original drawings and the
black outlines were drawn in machine-stitchery. Areas of colour and
texture were put in place using appliqué techniques. As you would
expect, the supporters have plenty to say, with advice to the players,
the referee and each other. The comments include (for the benefit of

146

non-Glaswegians) 'Nae borra' – no problem; 'Aw na! – Oh no!; 'Getinty him!' – Tackle him!; 'Skwerra ba orratime' – a highly technical instruction the meaning of which is lost on the authors. Of course, 1990 was the year of the World Cup in Italy and to mark this important event one of the supporters of Germany, the winning side, is lost amongst the crowd.

"Does anyone know any Boy Scouts?" was the desperate cry of Susan Green, the project co-ordinator. The husbands, brothers and boyfriends offered up as willing victims earlier in the year by women participants became more difficult to conscript as the time of reckoning drew near. By August, with only a handful of firm offers, we had to devise clever strategies. We made lists of potential sources of the male species, a diverting task and one which fascinated people who overheard us as we explored sporting, medical and hobby-based possibilities trying to target men who were good with their hands! Hence, Susan's public announcement at a *Keeping Glasgow in Stitches* workshop. We decided on greater stealth to save our reputations. Susan cornered Professor George, Head of Surgery at the Western Infirmary, at a charity ceilidh and he came with another surgeon to stitch for the day. It is whispered that he had to be shown how to thread a needle. Tony Higgins of the Scottish Football Association fielded two footballers from Clyde; Julian Spalding, Director, headed the team from Glasgow Museums; Summerlee Heritage Trust from Coatbridge did their stint with vigour; students from Glasgow School of Art; pupils from Kelvinside Academy and Kelvinhaugh Primary; veterans from Erskine Hospital; *Keeping Glasgow in Stitches* stalwarts Sergeant Graham and Alex Graham; Simon Fanshawe, the alternative comedian and TV presenter; students from Cardonald College and a visiting group from Macon, France, all made sure that the male sex was seen to take its responsibilities seriously and that the sewing would be done and done well.

So it was that the face in Malcolm McCormick's cartoon came to life in the unsteady but persistent hands of the male participants. Of course, there was a woman's guiding hand, Lesley Evans, helping them through the difficult bits, and it was left to the women to assemble the pieces with the unfailing support of Alex and Sergeant Graham.

When the banner was finished it was a bit too well done for some people's liking. The sea of grinning and grimacing faces fronted by the heroes Souness and McNeill, managers of Rangers and Celtic, testifies

CLYDE FOOTBALLERS
TRACE THEIR FANS —
AT LAST

to the historic importance of *Keeping Glasgow in Stitches* as both men moved to pastures new shortly afterwards. Between them, on the ball, is the logo of British Rail, representing British Railways Board Community Unit, sponsors for the month. At the top is a reminder of other sports and one of Glasgow's famous sons. The yacht in full sail is *Shamrock II*, one of the yachts in which Sir Thomas Lipton raced in his attempts to win the Americas Cup.

All those who took part in the making of this banner gave the public another treat. We had promised them men sewing and there was the 'new man' image tableaued in the central hall, suited figures bent over their embroidery, but we never did find the Boy Scouts.

148

MALCOLM
LOCHHEAD WITH
SOME OF THE
YOUNGEST
PARTICIPANTS FROM
KELVINHAUGH
PRIMARY SCHOOL
(*D. C. Thomson*)

"ALL RIGHT, YOU'VE
DONE WELL, NO
NEED TO LOOK
SMUG." STAFF FROM
SUMMERLEE
HERITAGE TRUST

'SUTURE SELF':
PROFESSOR DAVID
GEORGE AND
SURGEON PATRICK
O'DWYER COMPARE
KNOTS WHILE
ANDREW HAY SWOPS
HIS PAINTBRUSH FOR
A NEEDLE
(*D. C. Thomson*)

SHAMROCK III

GLASGOW FOOTBALL
Roddy Forsyth

In April 1989 a reader with the splendid name of J. M. Thunder, from Woking in Surrey, wrote to *The Times* to tell of the reaction he provoked while shopping in the town of Hania in Crete. He had, it seems, managed sufficient Greek to tell the shopkeepers he was from England. Mr Thunder then added: 'The response was immediate: "Dalglish! Dalglish!" This was apparently the only English the two Cretans knew.'

Leaving aside the fact that Mr Thunder might have varied the spelling of Cretan without losing the point of his story, his anecdote reminds us that if football is a kind of Esperanto then much of its vocabulary is rooted in Glasgow. Who, if they know the game, has not heard of its most famous rivals, Celtic and Rangers (not, incidentally, Glasgow Celtic and Glasgow Rangers, because there are no such beasts)? But how many realise that at the turn of the century Glasgow hosted the three greatest football stadia in the world in Ibrox, Parkhead and Hampden? Or that the Brazilians constructed the Maracana Stadium with a capacity of 200,000 to rob Hampden of its world crowd records?

If ever football classicists make a grand tour of the sport's origins they will begin in Glasgow where the crowds were of mythical proportions. Here are the football equivalents of the Parthenon, the Acropolis, and Parnassus, too. Anyone who doubts this should hoist themselves above the city on one of the helicopter flights which leave every few minutes from the pad in front of the Moat House Hotel.

The first landmark to arrest the gaze is immediately across the river in Govan, beyond the few remaining shipyard cranes which mark the corridor down which a quarter of all the world's shipping once steamed. The towering cantilever stands of Ibrox, home of Rangers, dominate the view southwards and the remarkable sweep of the main stand roof is supported by the longest free-standing steel girder in the world.

This fact is somehow typical of Rangers. To be the biggest, the loudest, the best; it comes with the turf. *We are the people*, their supporters boast. Rangers are perceived, by Scots who owe the club no allegiance, to be arrogant in success, resentful and often destructive in defeat. It is a cartoon image but the caricature is rooted in truth. For most of Rangers' history the team's supporters (along with their Celtic equivalents) indulged in periodic rampages in the manner of the Visigoths while the club's directors looked on like the geriatric Soviet leaders who used to assemble on the Red Square podium on May Day. There was not much jollity about the Ibrox board but there was a very great deal of complacency, which was abruptly shattered on 2 January 1971.

On that afternoon, a notably tranquil Rangers-Celtic match ended in improbable drama on the field. In the final minute Celtic took the lead only for their ancient rivals to equalise within seconds. At the first goal, swarms of Rangers supporters surged down Stairway 13 to leave the ground only to double back on their tracks at the sound of the equaliser. Someone slipped and the notoriously steep stairway became a killing ground as 66 spectators died in the crush and hundreds more were injured.

In the subsequent inquiry into the disaster Rangers were censured for ignoring warnings that the Ibrox exits were unsafe. The board embarked on the most radical option open to them and tore down the old stadium, replacing it with the present arena which, with an additional reconstruction of the main stand, can accommodate 52,000 spectators, more than half of whom are season-ticket holders.

Inside the ground are lavish executive boxes, franchised restaurants, conference suites and offices. Like Glasgow itself during the same period, Ibrox was transformed in the late 1970s and early 1980s and, like the city, Rangers were obliged to shed an unwholesome reputation for sectarian bigotry which had been exacerbated by the club's refusal to sign a Roman Catholic player knowingly. This outmoded taboo was blown apart on 10 July 1989 with the signing of Maurice Johnston, who was not merely a Catholic but a former Celtic player and one who only a few weeks earlier had promised to rejoin his old club before Rangers intervened with untold wages. And when the dust had settled on this parochial convulsion Rangers had the finest club stadium in Britain, the highest average attendance, the richest income. And if European success proved elusive, at home they were once again the biggest, the best. But, as their supporters would say, of course.

All that can be seen of the old Stairway 13 are a few steps set in

the concourse beyond the bottom right-hand corner of the ground, nearest to the river and the city centre. Near the opposite corner is a cluster of high-rise apartment buildings backing on to the M8. One of these was home to Kenny Dalgleish, idol of Greek island shopkeepers, but although he was a Rangers supporter within sight of Ibrox, Dalgleish was lured to the east end of the city to play for Celtic.

If we retrace Dalglish's route from the air it is easy to see the divide between the Glasgow of the image-makers and what might be called the unredeemed city, with its brew of vitality and dereliction. Celtic's proper name is the Celtic Football & Athletic Company Limited and the relevance of the latter part of the club's title is evident as you circle above Parkhead, where the football pitch is circumscribed by an elliptical shale running-track.

Celtic, traditionally the team of the Irish immigrants who flooded over to Scotland in the late 1800s, were unable to tap big business resources in the fashion of Rangers, and had to enter the last decade of the 20th century with a ground which – if the roofs were removed – would look almost exactly as it did a hundred years earlier. Not much had changed in its vicinity either, except for the demolition of the grim but awesome Parkhead Forge, which belonged to the Beardmore steelmaking family.

Like the vanished foundry, Parkhead – or Celtic Park, to use its official title – became a relic of a bygone era and a burden to a club forced by the Taylor Report, which followed the Hillsborough disaster in 1989, to upgrade their facilities at massive cost. To Rangers supporters, derisive in their custom-built comfort, Parkhead is a tip. To the Celtic faithful its homely, cavernous terracings have an ambience which is profoundly comforting. They yield pulsating memories. For perhaps five years after 1966, Parkhead quite simply provided the most exciting football entertainment in the world. Jock Stein, a Lanarkshire Protestant married to a Roman Catholic, guided the team to nine consecutive League titles and – in 1966–67 – Celtic won every trophy for which the team competed, an unmatched record at a level which saw Billy McNeill become the first British player to hoist the European Cup in triumph when he and his colleagues beat the fancied Inter Milan in Lisbon.

The achievement was even more remarkable in that the team was composed entirely of domestic talent, and there was scope for an extraordinary feat within days of the European Cup being brought

"We're investing in an all-seated stadium.. I've ordered a three-piece suite"

home to Glasgow when Rangers competed in the final of the European Cup Winners' Cup. They lost to Bayern Munich by the only goal of a game played on rather less than neutral territory in Nuremberg. Had Rangers won, Glasgow would have been the first city to possess the two principal European trophies at the same time.

In 1972 Glasgow hosted two European semi-finals simultaneously and by an uncanny turn of fate Celtic met Inter Milan, losing on penalty kicks after extra time, while Rangers beat Bayern Munich and went on to win the Cup Winners' Cup against Moscow Dynamo. On the evening when they both played, more than 160,000 watched the two games while something like 100 million joined in the fun on European television. There will never be another night like that because the rules of European football now forbid neighbouring teams to play on the same evening.

In all probability there will never be another date like 15 April 1970 either, when 136,505 watched (and on a Wednesday night) Celtic beat Leeds United at Hampden Park in a semi-final of the European Cup which set the attendance record for the tournament including the one for every final which has ever been played in any European tournament. The record for a final, needless to say, was also set at Hampden Park and just to prove that Glaswegians were not only partial to their own kind, 135,000 paid to see the highest scoring final when the fabulous Real Madrid shredded Eintracht Frankfurt 7–3 in 1963.

But then Hampden has entertained a litany of Biblical hosts . . . 149,547 for Scotland v England, April 1937, and, one week later, 146,433 for Celtic v Aberdeen . . . at a ground owned by Queen's Park, the only amateur side in the British professional leagues. Glasgow football delights in such paradoxes. Third Lanark, whose derelict ground may easily be inspected a few hundred yards from Hampden, paid their players from the club slot machines in 1967. Some of the wages went straight back to source but despite this brave attempt at perpetual motion the club went bankrupt shortly afterwards. Rangers may once have achieved 118,567 for yet another home game with Celtic, but on the same side of the river, humble Clyde managed a record gate of 52,000. Clyde have now abandoned Glasgow for a home in the hinterland but their stadium at Shawfield still exists, given over to greyhound racing. The city boundary runs across the pitch so perhaps Clyde always felt that they were being edged out. They did share with Partick Thistle for a couple of years, but since Partick

Thistle play in Maryhill and not Partick, Clyde were in serious danger of becoming schizophrenic. As indeed anyone is who chooses to get deeply involved with the mania of Glasgow football. Other sports are taken seriously in the city but only football is a genuine virulent obsession. Every day, in every Glaswegian bar, talk about the game accumulates like husks of plankton piling upon the ocean floor. Meanwhile, as the helicopter passengers return to their starting point on the river, they may glance to the north bank opposite Ibrox. There they will see the green oval of the West of Scotland Cricket ground, in Partick (where the Thistle do not play). It was on this field in 1872 that the world's first football international took place, a goalless draw between Scotland and England. It was from this place, half a century before Wembley rose up on empty Middlesex acres, that the good news of football spread to over 150 nations.

And that is why humble Cretan shopkeepers spoke with a Glasgow accent when they heard the sound of Thunder.

"Let's concentrate on qualifyin' fur the latter stages o' ra Glesca Cup"

SIR THOMAS LIPTON 1850–1931
Liz Arthur

Mention tea and the Americas Cup and most people will think of Sir Thomas Lipton. Sixty years after his fifth and last challenge, he is still remembered for sportsmanship and gallantry and his attempts to win the elusive cup.

This final defeat in 1930 was marked by the presentation of a gold cup inscribed:

> This symbol of a voluntary outpouring of Love, Admiration and Esteem is Presented to the Gamest Loser in the World of Sport. In the name of the Hundreds of Thousands of Americans and Wellwishers of Sir Thomas Johnston Lipton Bart KCVO.

The silver base is decorated with symbols of Fraternity, Integrity and Perseverance.

Lipton developed his passion for the sea and ships as a 14-year-old cabin boy working on one of the Burns liners sailing between the Broomielaw and Belfast. However, it was not until later in life, when he had established a business empire, that he was able to pursue his sporting career.

It was during his four-year stay in America, working on tobacco plantations, and at other odd jobs in a prosperous grocery, that his lifelong affection for the country and its people grew. He also laid the foundations for his future success through his growing understanding of commercial enterprise before returning to Glasgow in 1869 with savings of $500, a barrel of flour and a rocking-chair for his mother. His parents had emigrated from Northern Ireland to the West of Scotland to escape the great potato famine and ran a very small grocery shop in Crown Street. In 1871 Lipton opened his own first shop, Lipton Market in Stobcross Street, selling high quality provisions at reasonable prices. By cutting out the middleman, and through careful organisation and shrewd marketing, particularly his inventive use of

A LIPTON SHOP IN
THE 1920S

advertising, business thrived. Lipton Markets spread throughout
Britain and his goods were sold worldwide. In 1890 tea was introduced
with the slogan 'Direct from the tea garden to the teapot'. This firmly
established his empire and 'Lipton' became a household name, but it
was through his charitable work and most of all as a sportsman that
the man himself became well known.

By now a millionaire, he was able to indulge his love of sailing. In
1898 he bought a Clyde-built steam yacht and renamed her *Erin*. She
was later to be used to provide lavish entertainment for King Edward
VII. Lipton issued his first challenge for the Americas Cup the following
year in the first of his succession of five racing yachts named *Shamrock*.
Numbers *I* and *III* were designed by the famous Scottish designer
William Fife, but only *Shamrocks II* and *III* were Clyde-built at
William Denny & Bros. *Shamrock IV* came closest to winning the Cup
in 1920. She was designed and built at Camper & Nicholson in
Portsmouth, as was the majestic *Shamrock V*, a new 'J' class of boat of
which only ten were ever built.

Lipton's yachts were extremely successful in British and European
waters and it was through his yachting exploits that he won the
friendship and support of the king. He received many honours during

SIR THOMAS LIPTON
WITH SOME OF HIS
YACHTING TROPHIES

his lifetime and his support of various charities was recognised with a knighthood in 1898 and a baronetcy in 1902. Glasgow also honoured him in 1923 with the Freedom of the City.

Although Lipton moved his headquarters to London in 1894 he never forgot his native Glasgow and recalled his childhood with pleasure. On his death in 1931 the boy who had left St Andrew's Parish School at the age of ten to take his first job as an errand boy bequeathed his entire estate (with the exception of Osidge, his London home), worth almost £1 million, to the city for the relief of the poor. Most of his trophies are in the collection of Glasgow Museums.

IT'S NAILED FAST!
Sir Thomas—I've come to lift the Cup.

OCTOBER

Jane Carroll and Alistair McCallum studied at Glasgow School of Art. Their company, Central Designs, produces a wide range of work. They took photographs and made drawings which were developed into a collage to create an interesting atmosphere.

OCTOBER
The Big City

There had to be one panel of real atmosphere in the set of 12 and October with its theme of the 'big city' became that panel. We are slipping into winter, the nights are drawing in and the idea was developed of having people set against a city skyline to evoke the feeling of Glasgow at night, on a Friday after the pubs have emptied.

Glasgow is held to have some of the finest Victorian architecture in Europe and as 1990 was a celebration of Glasgow it seemed important to refer to some of its fine buildings. At the top is an amalgam of Glasgow's towers and spires, including the Cathedral, Trinity and the University. Their outline is set against a stunningly dramatic autumn sunset which is a regular feature of this season in Glasgow. Malcolm remembers driving into the city from the east, dazzled by a vivid sunset and almost leaving the road trying to work out how such superb colour could be interpreted in textiles. The effect was finally achieved by building up layers of chiffons and net to create the right degree of luminosity.

The brief for the inner banner was that it should show the loneliness of the big city. Jane Carroll and Alistair McCallum from Cranhill Arts/Central Design chose to look at Glasgow from a shadowy viewpoint. To show the rain and a wet backstreet somewhere near the river, a street-light, just out of sight, picks out a couple in close embrace. Framed in fluorescent threads they snatch a lustful moment between the fish and chips and the last cigarette. The drawing of the forms and detail was executed in virtuoso machine-embroidery under the direction of Kim Paterson of NeedleWorks, who also supervised the creation of shadowy textures for the buildings from a bewildering array of rich and exotic fabrics. At first there were problems. How do we create the effect of a pavement oiled by heavy rain, of the distressed wood of the lock-up, of the solid concrete of the Kingston Bridge, or the rain-slicked buildings and the night-lit windows of a tenement?

DETAIL

162

Gradually, the inventive use of plastic and trapping threads between layers of semi-transparent fabrics gave the variety of textures we were looking for and the banner took its shape and mood from them. Fluorescent yarns, black lurex thread, shisha glass and luminous ribbon all help accentuate the slightly eerie coldness and the electric atmosphere. Even the group themselves were surprised by the potency of the effects they created.

To balance the mood, a plain informative codicil, a map of the city, was included to give an indication of scale and of the towns which make up its conurbation. The map, with the River Clyde at its heart, is worked in counted thread techniques. The original drawing showed the names drawn in small neat lettering but this created the problem of producing sewable letters of the correct scale to fit the overall size of the map. There was a painful morning during which a great deal of graph paper was wasted as non-mathematicians struggled with the calculations. At this point one of the miracles of the project occurred in the form of Caroline Levitt, a participant who confessed to being a

SO THAT'S HOW YOU DO LAZY DAISY! KIM PATERSON, WORKSHOP LEADER, LEARNS SOMETHING NEW

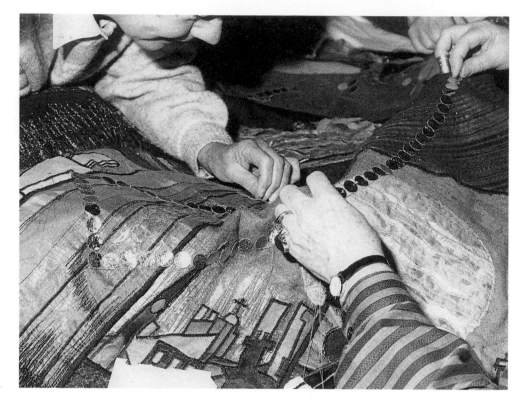

DOING A NUMBER

mathematician by training and who duly produced all the words accurately to scale in a very short time. Visitors constantly complained that we had missed out their home area. We struggled to oblige, whenever we could, but if the name of your area is missing we apologise – time conspired against us.

As with the May banner the large number breaks into the inner banner area. In order not to shatter the atmosphere the number was outlined using small discs of 22-carat, gold-coated kid. Another link between the two areas was achieved by bringing fiery, hot smoke from the chimney out through the number and up to meet the setting sun's reflection in the Clyde. All that remained was to find a place for the sponsor's logo. After careful consideration the Clydesdale Bank PLC positioned its logo in the form of a sign on the gable-end of a building.

DESIGNERS JANE
CARROLL AND
ALASTAIR McCALLUM
EXAMINE THE
FINISHED WORK

THE LIGHT IN HERE IS
NO BETTER!

NIGHT
William Hunter

Where prostitutes and poets have trodden the night streets alone, everybody else needs a pal. Even the constabulary learned early it takes two to tangle with the city after dark. Glasgow's best companion for midnight rambles called himself Shadow. He was an unsleeping watcher of the down-side of town. His patch was Argyle Street and the tenebrous backlands of Trongate and Saltmarket. Shadow supped in shebeens and improved his nights in cop stations, low pie shops and twilight stews. Once he went with a sad whore to her lair. It cost him plenty to get clean away. (For *his* minder Shadow had a detective or sometimes patrolled the sin streets with a low-life newspaper reporter.)

In a little book called *Midnight Scenes and Social Photographs* (1858) Shadow wrote all about it. No scholarly statistical account has since come close to his picture of the gaudy life on the city's seamy-side. Shadow (his name was Alexander Brown and his day job was a printer) fancied himself invisible. He used an I-am-a-camera technique to take his night pictures of people too ugly to go out when the sun shone. 'There a fight has commenced,' he wrote, 'between three of the lowest thieves and prostitutes – drunk and too disfigured at an earlier hour to walk the streets.' He decided that night people were different from ordinary pedestrians:

> Pent up in their hovels all day, they come out just to breathe a mouthful of fresh air before laying themselves down on beds of rags and straw. It is a city that these poor people have not the moral courage to venture out during the day, while the sun might rejoice their hearts, and ventilate their unwholesome garments.

Although Shadow reported that only poor sinners – 'like cockroaches' as he put it – promenaded by gaslight, he saw beauty in the night. He enjoyed gawping at passers-by for whom life was too short to live it only by day. He found exhilarating street folk who wanted to keep singing, shouting, shopping and seeing each other so long as they could stay on their feet. And he saw a city of light that the poets had missed, being solitary creatures and unsighted by how sensitive they are.

Glasgow has had a thin time in poesy. Hugh MacDiarmid found it an awfu' place. It wearied him. A cloud of dust fell on his thoughts. The fog was infernal and broth-like. To Kenneth White in a nocturnal poem the night city was a blues tune played on a mournful trombone. He saw fog and rain and mud and grease. Shadow saw light. Even at the river's murky harbour he noted:

> The rain has subsided, the heavens have lost their dull lowering, and the twinkling little stars of the night are all but transparent through a yet hazy sky. Despite the sable curtain which overhangs the Clyde, the waters are yet suffused with light.

Foggy nights in Shadow's time were roofed by a sky glare from the furnaces of Dixon's Blazes, pig-ironworks at Govanhill. In a sooty way they held back the dark hours. From such industrial garishness was learned how not to accept night as a dark bowl. Some loyalists still never weary of remembering that Glasgow's main post office became bulb-lit before London's. When Lord Kelvin's house went all-electric it ignited a beacon around the world. Now in a handful of years the night city has become operatic. Floodlighting of the architecture has added lofty sparkle to the dogged jollity of the streets. To a cityscape of good dignity, decent style and weighty beauty has been added scattered brilliance. In the gloaming, the Mitchell Library becomes an ornate Cunarder on a moonlight voyage, while Glasgow University's fierce hauteur turns into a Wagnerian fantasy. Even John Knox on his Necropolis plinth has got all lit up. Dear God, under its illuminated harbour bridges the very river seems alive.

To reawaken the city from the zombie torpor into which it had fallen took many princely kisses. Lively enterprise in the City Chambers speeded the renaissance. Cherishing old tenement houses helped much. The enshrining of the Burrell Collection in its own parkland temple was an elegant resuscitator. Above all it was the refusal of the night people, especially the young ones, to accept defeat that revived ancient Glesca. The weary old place was saved by its night people. They rekindled its light by how they refused to leave the streets.

An exact emotional date can be put on the rebirth – September 1973. And the monument to the arisen city was a ramshackle palace of varieties known as the Apollo. Once it had been a behemoth picture house, the biggest in Europe, called Green's Playhouse, and now it is a hole in the ground. Out of its crumbling walls tottered the new Glasgow, mothered and fathered by travellers from afar. Among its early kiss-of-life revivers were Johnny Cash, the Rolling Stones, and Diana Ross. They endured conditions so bleak that when Duke Ellington gave a band concert a gas heater had to play alongside his piano to unfreeze his fingers. So the Apollo filled the streets again with regular crowds who were noisy and excited for more reasons than football. Around its rickety hub, and usually operated by the same free-wheeling impresarios, whirled new whizzo pubs and discos. In the temporary way of the stage props of young entertainment, the Muscular Arms, Electric Garden, the Ultratheque have all been shifted from the scene. Their legacy lingers. They pioneered late nights which were followed by grander celebrations. Of any enduring benefits brought by the official festivals of culture and arts (and of gardens), however, the most palpable was only to rewrite the licensing laws to suit night-life tastes which stay-awake Apollo people had rediscovered for themselves. By instinct, young Glasgow had appreciated that if the city failed to live in its streets it might not live at all. From the outer limbs of the housing schemes they kept the blood pumping at the heart of town.

Shadow had been there before them. While he marvelled at the number of pubs, he was also appalled. He pondered what a Jerusalem it would be if every city-centre drinking hole had a church spire. Yet he warmed to the lust for brightness they contained – their flaring gaslights and frosted globes. Granite fountains added night tranquillity. About the many-mirrored walls he reflected: 'Everybody seems to have turned out to look at each other.' He noted the enthusiasm of the poorest people – 'the lowest orders' as he called them – to get all dressed up. He wrote:

> Time and drink work wonders. The face but a few minutes since so long and doleful has now become like others in the company luminous as a sunbeam.

Glasgow at its most vital is a city of night sunbeams. From Dixon's ironworks was learned how to blaze away the dark hours. From the crummy beginnings of Shadow's shebeens and slum bordellos, nighttown became the dancingest and mostest picture-going pleasure place in all Britain. Even statistically, there was no touching it for its acreage of palais de danse floor-space or square footage of cinema screen. For style, the new city has still to catch up with the old. It has yet to recapture the kind of flamboyance that adorned one picture palace, called the Norwood, with a replica of the Forth Railway Bridge on its canopy and filled with happy feet vibrating hangar-like Dennistoun Palais. In dance-halls, never in pubs, was developed not just quickness of heel and toe but fleet tongues. At the Locarno, Green's ballroom, the F & F, the Albert, and in bare side-street sheds was perfected the city's own peppery local lingo and patter. "Wull ye burl the other way," a damsel would learn to cry. "You're unscrewing ma wooden leg."

While night people made pungent the city's language, they also personified a vagrant desperation. So much life happened in the streets because so little could happen in mean homes. Only outside was there room to move. Only in public places could there be privacy. It took Shadow to separate a jollier ingredient in the gift for making night and day a continuous programme, especially at the end of every week which he liked to write in exclamatory italics – *'Saturday!'* Then sleep came only when money ran out. As he saw it, the street party ended for the single reason he called 'a want of siller'. Until that sad moment arrived, nights were illuminated by cash burning holes in pockets. There was elated determination to start every new week dead broke. Tomorrow, far from never coming, *was* today, especially if it was *Saturday!*

Tired but not wanting to go home, crowds lingered in Argyle Street, even only to gaze at bright shop windows, 'with manifest discomfort at having money in their pockets' quoth Shadow. When poor, which has been most of the time, golden nights are beyond Glasgow. This city's good old gift is to enjoy itself up to the limits of its wherewithal by the light of a moon that is silvery. Shadow showed first how its street spectaculars outshone even its theatre nights, even a winter pantomime, even at the old Princess's in the Gorbals across the river from where Shadow walked.

**A SOUP KITCHEN IN
THE CITY CENTRE**
(*Christopher Nicoletti*)

**THE CLYDE AND THE
KINGSTON BRIDGE**
(*Christopher Nicoletti*)

ENTERTAINMENT —
THE CINEMA
(*Christopher Nicoletti*)

GORDON STREET TAXI
RANK
(*Christopher Nicoletti*)

THE MITCHELL
LIBRARY AND M8
MOTORWAY
(*Christopher Nicoletti*)

BOTHWELL STREET
(*Christopher Nicoletti*)

**A NIGHT ON THE
TOWN**
(*Christopher Nicoletti*)

HENRY AFRIKA DISCO
(*Glasgow Herald*)

LATE NIGHT, GOOD NIGHT (*Christopher Nicoletti*)

NOVEMBER

Malcolm Lochhead studied embroidery at Glasgow School of Art. Widely experienced in many fields of design he is a lecturer in Design at Queen's College and was responsible for the overall design and colour scheme, also for the complete November banner.

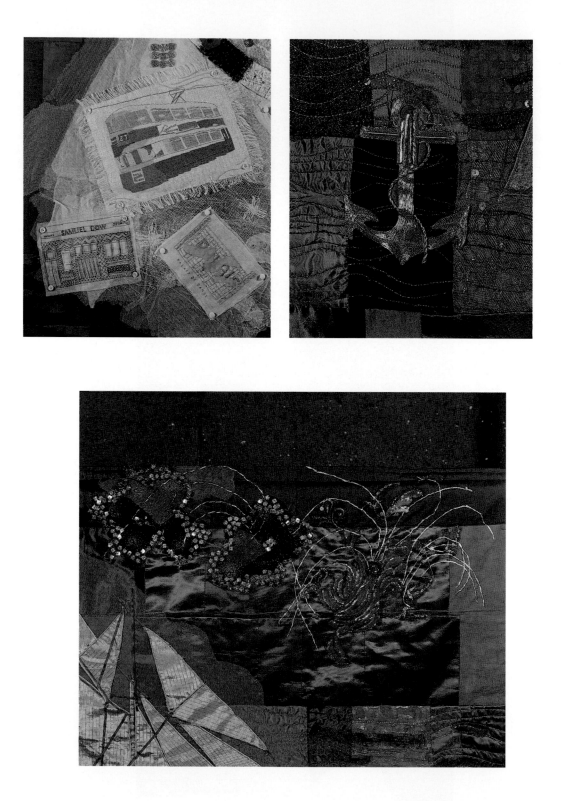

NOVEMBER

Remembrance

November's banner is the only one of the 12 which was designed by one person, Malcolm Lochhead, who chose the theme of remembrance which allowed the examination of some of the things which Glasgow has lost and regrets.

The upper part of the banner follows the format of the others and has a rich dark Clyde flowing across it with another yacht, this time the *Glennifer*, built in 1899 for James Coats. This forms a link with the Coats Leisure Crafts Group, the sponsor for this banner, and with Glasgow Museums, who have in their collection one of the special sweaters worn by the crew of the *Glennifer*. The goldwork anchor in the river is the company's symbol and was exquisitely worked by the embroideress Hannah Frew Paterson.

As it is November the sky is alight with fireworks in metallic threads and velvet. Fireworks were an integral part of the Year of Culture as the celebrations began with massive displays all around the city.

The number 9 contains the first clue to the meaning of the design. It is overlaid with a black tulle question mark posing the question 'Why have we lost so much in Glasgow?' The other reference is the white disc whose long tail forms the letter Q, another metaphor for the question.

The inner banner, which is not clearly delineated, is the only abstract image of the 12. The curved lines receding into the distance represent the centuries moving back towards the year 1176 when Glasgow received its Charter. The tail of the Q represents the mists of time which have caught up images associated with the city and is swirling them away into the past and out of memory.

Each of the arc shapes, which form a skeleton of time, was cut from stiff interlining which was wrapped with fabric and yarns of graduated darkening tones. These in turn were enriched with surface

NAN, ISABEL, MOLLY
AND SHEILA PUT
THEIR BACKS INTO
THE WORK

stitchery. The biggest arc, which represents the 20th century, was divided into decades represented by ribbon divisions with appropriate dates and then subdivided into years. You will find two black areas, the First and Second World Wars. The poppy is in remembrance of the citizens of Glasgow who died in both.

The annual divisions allowed the participants to make personal nostalgic statements. Some marked marriages, others birthdays or bereavements, with tiny embroidered gold symbols tucked away privately among the textures. One young participant made a mark of undying love in the 1990 section only to return shortly afterwards demanding to unpick the symbol as the affair had ended prematurely.

A group of students from Queen's College was sent out with a questionnaire to discover the things Glasgow's citizens missed most. Some strong favourites quickly emerged, including men-only pubs, the great dance-halls, Italian cafés and, most frequently mentioned, the tramcar. There were some unexpected regrets, like the lack of civility or lack of parking spaces. Some elderly folk regretted that they had not

had a better education. Others said that they had no regrets and thought the city was much better now than in their youth – proof positive that for some Glasgow's definitely Miles Better.

The images were worked using techniques such as shadow work, fabric printing and painting. They are deliberately pale to represent the fading of memories. The tramcar is made in counted thread techniques. The little pictures were worked separately, held in place with buttons so that should something return the image can be unbuttoned from the banner. The background was interpreted by the participants from Malcolm's crayon drawing into an exquisite surface texture of machine- and hand-embroidery.

As the project neared its close there was a rush of people determined not to be left out, as well as those who had become *Keeping Glasgow in Stitches* addicts and the backbone of the project dedicated to ensuring that all was perfect. Others had become devoted followers of Malcolm Lochhead, regularly attending the Monday workshops to learn the intricacies of design and ingenious ways of creating subtle

JIM CLARK OF COATS
LEISURE CRAFTS AND
HANNAH FREW
PATERSON, WITH
PARTICIPANTS AND
BYSTANDERS,
INSPECT THE
FINISHED BANNER

effects and textures. They were not going to miss the opportunity and inspiration of working on his banner, even knowing that his rigorous standards would demand perfection. He admitted that the working of November was a nerve-wracking experience as it was necessary to entrust his fragile concept to so many people. However, they worked with serious and skilled intent and the results of their labours far exceeded his wildest expectations.

November, the banner of remembrance, was almost complete and everyone associated with it will remember those final frantic weeks of *Keeping Glasgow in Stitches* when record numbers of participants beavered away on both the November and December banners. As time began to run out we increasingly heard phrases such as "I'm just going to take this home to . . .", "Maybe if we just machine rather than . . ." The Tron clock on the December panel was beginning to tick its way to the final hour.

WHIT'S THE MAITTER WI' GLASGOW?

Joseph Farrell

When the American comedienne and filmstar Whoopi Goldberg visited Glasgow to perform at the first ever Mayfest, she reacted with surprise to being complimented by taxi driver after taxi driver not on the quality of her show but on her sheer courage in daring to set foot in Glasgow at all. "Glesca's goat an awfy reputation," she recalled being told by great bears of men, awestruck at the fact that this petite, black figure had had the pluck to leave Chicago for such a savage place as unreformed Glasgow.

Ms Goldberg remained nonplussed, not because in the entire duration of her stay had she failed to see those rivers of blood which, her interlocutors implied, regularly stained George Square or Sauchiehall Street red, but for a reason which was infinitely more wounding to civic pride. She was quite simply unaware that Glasgow had any reputation at all, whether for casual violence or, in its reformed state, for cultural excellence. To the amazement of one and all, the 'No Mean City' image of which they were, in a perverse but very real way, proud, had simply not crossed the Atlantic. That was devastating – for the Glaswegian.

It is perfectly forgivable to denigrate or demean Glasgow. The sin against the Holy Ghost lies in not being aware of its special dualities, in failing to regard it as unique and inimitable in some way or another. Exactly which way is altogether secondary. It can be viewed as uniquely violent or uniquely friendly, as the home of Rennie Mackintosh or of the razor kings, as the epitome of unparalleled architectural taste or a desert of philistine tastelessness. On any night of the year, when the patrons of the pubs are spilling on to the streets, there are Glaswegians who will talk in any of those terms, and sometimes in all simultaneously. The essential thing is to give the city a central place in the scheme of things and to talk of it in superlatives – any superlatives.

Glasgow has always been a curiously self-absorbed city, oscillating between self-excoriation and self-preening, but always self-aware and self-orientated. A traveller returning from the Himalayas or from the Andes could regale his public with tales of foreign ways, but when it came to questions he would always be asked to explain what the local people thought of Glasgow. It was the unquestioned assumption of Glasgow's doctors of divinity, architects and engineers that what they did was the subject of heated, perhaps hostile, debate in climes and in idioms whose existence they could only guess at.

Glasgow's self-image reflected that notion of itself as central. Nostalgia is a record of how people believe they were, and no dry-as-dust historian has any role in that inner chronicle. Glasgow nostalgia is not necessarily romantic or idealising. There is a legend in Glasgow to cover every aspect of life. Glasgow used to have more music-halls per head than any other city in Britain. Tommy Morgan used to say that he could go and see a different show each week for 19 weeks and get to each one by tramcar. Glasgow once had the most thriving socialist movement in Britain, if not Europe. Glasgow has more parkland than any other city. The Red Clydesiders, Harry McShane, John McGovern and Davy Kirkwood could fill cinemas on a Sunday night. If you are tired of Glasgow you are tired of life, as Doctor Johnson failed to say.

At the same time, they say, Glasgow had the most abominable housing conditions of any place in mainland Britain. An English journalist of genius, William Bolitho, wrote a pamphlet entitled *Cancer of Empire* exposing the scandal of the slums. Glasgow had a record of infant mortality which compared with Calcutta. Rickets and TB were rife in the tenement areas of the city. Glasgow was Europe's most violent city, ruled by the open razor mobs until Lord Carmont crushed them with heavy sentences at the High Court. 'No Mean City' was a mild version of the truth. There used to be menacing graffiti on the walls which said things like 'TOI YA BASS!' Glasgow's streets are not safe to walk on, especially after dark, even if Glasgow people are the most open and friendly you could hope to meet . . .

Glasgow belongs to anyone with the imagination to choose those elements of the past which make most appeal to their individual taste. It seems set to disappear under the weight of the legends to which it has given birth, with the one point of convergence being that there was a more dramatic, more authentic Glasgow which was simply allowed to disappear – there is even a book with that title – *The City That Disappeared*. The poet and songwriter Adam McNaughton wrote the sentimental/nostalgic piece about the way we supposedly were, 'The Glasgow that I used to know':

> Oh where is the Glasgow where I used tae stey,
> The white wally closes done up wi' pipe clay;
> Where ye knew every neighbour frae first flair to third,
> And to keep your door locked was considered absurd.

In keeping with Glasgow's variation of Newton's law – that every positive statement about the city will encounter an equal and opposite splutter of contemptuous denial – Jim McLean weighed in with a witty, bitter parody highlighting an alternative face of old Glasgow:

> Where is the Glasgow I used to know?
> The tenement buildings that let in the snow,
> Through cracks in the plaster the cold wind did blow,
> And the water we washed in was fifty below.

Glasgow is as prone today to nostalgia epidemics as it once was to outbreaks of cholera or 'fever'. No doubt this is due to the sense of alienation or disorientation that people of the post-war generations feel in a city which changed out of all recognition. After the war the official policy was not to develop or restore Glasgow but to replace it. Some folk were shuttled out to new towns like East Kilbride or Cumbernauld, others to the periphery housing estates which quickly became a by-word all over Europe for the impact of the unfeeling intrusions of planners on people's lives. The city centre was despoliated or destroyed. There was, in retrospect, something uniquely perverse (how easy it is to fall into this swagger) about this deliberate attempt to destroy all continuity. To say this is not to fall into sentimentality over the 'golden community' of tenement living. The people most prone to that cloying mood today are those who never had to use a stairhead cludgie or inhabit a single-end. The fact remains that nowhere else (absolutely nowhere!) was there so little concern over the maintenance of some form of link with the past. When the great bell-tower in St Mark's Square in Venice collapsed in the early years of the century, the slogan of people and authorities alike was to have it replaced 'Com'era, dov'era' – 'As it was, where it was'. Similarly, when Hitler's bombers had flattened Warsaw, the first task of the restored Polish government was to rebuild the city as the citizens remembered it. They even used the paintings of the Italian cityscape artist, Bellotto, to ensure authenticity.

Glasgow pulled itself apart. Nobody else did it. There really used to be a cross at Charing Cross – not just a motorway flyover. (By the same token it can confidently be predicted that in a couple of years there will be a bout of nostalgia for the Charing Cross as it briefly was in the '60s and '70s when you could see the Mitchell Library, before they allowed Them to build that absurd, rose-coloured creation on top of the bridge that used to go nowhere.) There used to be a Grand Hotel there, as elsewhere there used to be the Alhambra Theatre, The Empire, the grand Christian Institute building in Bothwell Street. Real people used to live in what is now the Merchant City, or all along Parliamentary Road and down in the Gorbals. In many cases, it was right and proper that they disappeared. Ralph Glasser, with his books recalling the Jewish community in the Gorbals of his boyhood, writes beautifully about that benighted area, and in every case it was disconcerting for those who grew up in a particular place to find it had been willed out of existence. Such districts carried a weight of personal associations which can never be recaptured or conveyed by any other means. To stare at an empty space, or even at a reflecting-glass office-block, which is associated with an individual past – with childhood games, with first love – brings on an inevitable sense of loss. It may also induce that pleasing sense of melancholy which makes run-of-the-mill adults believe for a moment that they are more feeling, more given to strong emotion, more in contact with depths of thinking than they know they are. That is one function of nostalgia.

The other is to provide reassurance. Glasgow suffered another flood of nostalgia in 1990 at exactly the moment when the city authorities wanted to celebrate the New Glasgow. It does not matter whether there was anything really new about it, or whether the newness was a PR bluff; the fact is, that talk was of a new post-industrial civilisation, of the regenerated Merchant City, and many people felt outsiders in that vision of things. In general, the city's writers turned their backs on the 'new' reality and preferred to cater for the dispossessed and the excluded, to create/recreate an image of Glasgow in its great days when it was an industrial centre. Bill Bryden's *The Ship*, Bryan Elsley's *Govan Ghost Story* and Tony Roper's *Paddy's Market* are all works which look at a city which has disappeared as completely

as the tram. It is a nostalgia very similar to the belief of the old woman in Tony Roper's supremely nostalgic *The Steamie* that, when she was a girl, the warm days of summer lasted all the way from May to September. Nostalgia edits out of memory all the grating sequences. Nostalgia is a distorting mirror. Nostalgia is a tear shed on the grave of long dead parents, not because we miss them any longer but because we yearn for the recurrence of the opportunities available to us when they were there and we were young. No city, in no country, at no point of history is as prone to nostalgia as Glasgow now. How could they be?

CHARING CROSS WITH THE GRAND HOTEL

HOEY'S SHOP,
SPRINGBURN ROAD,
1920S
(*Springburn Museum
Trust*)

A CLYDESIDE
WELDER, 1940S
(*British Council war
photograph*)

THE *QUEEN MARY*
BEING FITTED OUT,
CLYDEBANK

PS *COLUMBA* ON THE
CLYDE

THE GLASGOW THAT I USED TO KNOW
Adam McNaughton

Oh where is the Glasgow where I used tae stey?
The white wally closes done up wi' pipe cley,
Where ye knew every neighbour frae first floor to third,
And to keep your door locked was considered absurd.
Do you know the folk steyin' next door to you?

And where is the wee shop where I used to buy
A quarter o' totties, a tuppenny pie,
A bag o' broken biscuits an three tottie scones?
And the wumman aye asked, 'How's your maw gettin' on?'
Can your big supermarkets gie service like that?

And where is the wean that wance played in the street,
Wi' a jorrie, a peerie, a gird wi' a cleek?
Can he still cadge a hudgie or dreep aff a dyke?
Or is writin' on wa's noo the wan thing he likes?
Can he tell chickie-mellie fae hunch-cuddy-hunch?

And where is the tramcar that wance did the ton
Up the Great Western Road on the old Yoker run?
The conductress aye knew how to deal wi' a nyaff,
'If ye're gaun then get oan, if ye're no then get aff!'
Are there ony like her on the buses the day?

And where is the chip shop that I knew sae well?
The wee corner café where they used to sell
Hot peas and brey and Macallums and pokes,
An ye knew they were Tallies the minute they spoke:
'Dae ye wanta da raspberry ower yer ice-a-cream?'

Oh where is the Glasgow that I used to know?
Big Wullie, Wee Shooie, the steamie, the Co?
The shilpit wee bauchle, the glaikit big dreep,
The ba' on the slates, and yer gas in a peep?
If ye scrape the veneer aff, are these things still there?

TEDDY DESMOND'S
SYMPHONIC
SYNCOPATORS
OUTSIDE THE
DENNISTOUN PALAIS,
1930

BOOK BARROW BY ST
ANDREW-BY-THE-
GREEN CHURCH

TRAMS IN UNION STREET, LATE 1930S

LAMPLIGHTER, THE LADYWELL FLATS BEHIND DUKE STREET, MARCH 1976
(Malcolm R. Hill, Partick Camera Club)

THE LAST TRAM,
4 SEPTEMBER 1962

ICE-CREAM CART,
HIGH COURT, 1959
(*Malcolm R. Hill*)

FAREWELL TO GLASGOW
Words and music by Jim McLean

Where is the Glasgow I used to know?
The tenement buildings that let in the snow.
Through the cracks in the plaster the cold wind did blow.
And the water we washed in was fifty below.

We read by the gaslight, we had nae TV,
Hot porridge for breakfast, cold porridge for tea,
Some weans had rickets and some had TB,
Aye, that's what the Glasgow of old means to me.

Noo the neighbours complained if we played wi' a ba',
Or hunch-cuddy-hunch against somebody's wa',
If we played kick-the-can we'd tae watch for the law,
And the polis made sure we did sweet bugger a'.

And we huddled together to keep warm in bed,
We had nae sheets or blankets, just auld coats instead,
And a big balaclava to cover your head,
And 'God, but it's cold' was the only prayer said.

Noo there's some say that tenement living was swell,
That's the wally-close toffs who had doors wi' a bell,
Two rooms and a kitchen and a bathroom as well,
While the rest of us lived in a single-end hell.

So wipe aff that smile when you talk o' the days,
Ye lived in the Gorbals or Cowcaddens ways,
Remember the rats and the mice ye once chased,
For tenement living was a bloody disgrace.

Published by J. B. Music

DECEMBER

June Chrisfield Chapman studied wood engraving and illustration at Glasgow School of Art. For December she wanted to encapsulate the atmosphere of the Scottish theatre with as many characters, both past and present, as possible.

DECEMBER

Entertainment

With the December banner we have almost come full circle. The atmosphere is again cold and frosty but there is a feeling of expectancy in the air. The River Clyde flows relentlessly on, rather like time itself, and as the December group worked on, the bag and baggage of *Keeping Glasgow in Stitches* was dismantled around them. Material was folded and stored, threads rewound and designs rolled away. With only two weeks to go, the launch of the banners was being organised and the 11 that had been completed were being given their final grooming.

The clock on the Tolbooth tower is showing three minutes to midnight and 1990 is about to slip into the past. Everyone is waiting for the bells to ring in the New Year, glasses are charged and shortly the age-old toast will be spoken, "Here's tae us wha's like us", followed by the riposte "Damn few and they're a' deid!"

December's banner was created under tremendous pressure. It was designed by June Chrisfield Chapman, the choice of Billy Differ, Manager of the King's Theatre, who was invited to select the artist. It was a nail-biting task to recreate the painted portraits of well-known characters in textiles without losing each individual likeness. Without the unfailing patience and guidance of Lesley Evans the participants might not have achieved such a convincing piece of work. The faces are a combination of paint, thread, fabric and net.

Set in the Kings Theatre, on a brightly lit stage, are the ghostly stars of the past with Harry Lauder at the centre. Swinging from a trapeze high above them are that well-loved duo Francie and Josie, created by Rikki Fulton and Jack Milroy. Ringed around the foreground is a selection of Scottish stars who have graced Glasgow theatres. Anti-clockwise from top left we have Kenneth McKellar, Andy Stewart, Stanley Baxter, Walter Carr, Billy Connolly, Una McLean, Johnnie Beattie and Chic Murray. In the middle-distance is a

193

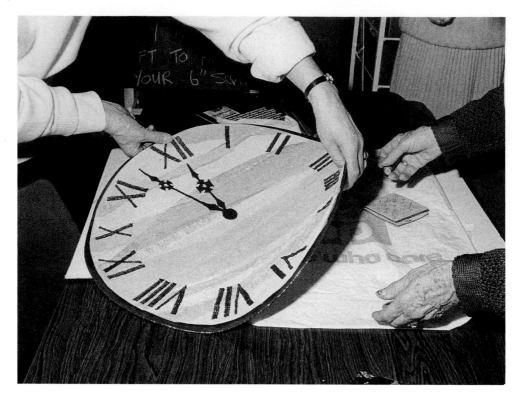

TIME RUNS OUT FOR
*KEEPING GLASGOW IN
STITCHES*. THE
HANDS AND
NUMERALS WERE
MADE BY THE LACE
GROUP

bevy of lovelies singing 'Auld Lang Syne', from left to right Fran
and Anna, Janet Brown and Lulu. We know they are singing this
song because, in the best pantomime tradition, the bouncing ball is
following the words on the 'cloot'. At Glasgow pantomimes when
audience participation was required the cast would call out "Bring
doon the cloot", and the cloot (cloth) with the words would then be
lowered.

There are some exquisite details on this banner which might pass
unnoticed, such as the clock face, which was made by the Glasgow
Lace Group, and Stanley Baxter's lilac wig, confected from specially
dyed unspun floss silk. He is holding a piece of 'paper' bearing the
arms of the Trades House of Glasgow who made a generous donation
to the project, while Walter Carr has a *Glasgow Herald* to represent
the December sponsor.

On an evening in early December we joined Liz Arthur and Susan
Green in the Art Gallery. Side by side the banners were laid out on the

VIEW FROM THE
GODS

floor for inspection. Julian Spalding joined us and we all trouped upstairs to see, for the first time, the effect of the work. Mingled with a sense of pride was the greater sensation of relief. The banners, the result of a great deal of love, commitment and humour, were simply wonderful.

Saturday 8 December was the final day of the project. It was a day like any other, busy and gregarious with people stitching the last stitches of the December panel. At 4 p.m. we had champagne provided by Malcolm, but no great speeches. There was an atmosphere of sadness, rather than celebration, that the project had come to an end. Putting aside half-drunk glasses, participants began to clear away, savouring the last moments in the museum which had become their home for a year.

However, it wasn't over yet. During the previous weeks the launch of *Keeping Glasgow in Stitches* had been organised in secret by Clare Higney. With invitations sent out to 800 people and the dictum to bring a cushion, the launch had to be as special as the work itself. And

JIMMY CHISHOLM
AND JOHNNIE BETT
ENTERTAIN WITH
THEIR PANTO
ROUTINE AT THE
UNVEILING OF THE
BANNERS,
16 DECEMBER 1990
(*Alan Crumlish*)

so it was that at 6.30 on the evening of 16 December about 800 people sat expectantly on the floor of the central hall in the Art Gallery and Museum.

The music of the 'Song of the Clyde' was heard and, as the spotlight hit the January banner, singer/songwriter Ewan McVicar treated us to his version of 'The No. 33 Bus'. For February 'Spin and Weave' was sung in Urdu and Scots as a haunting duet, and on we went with three pensioners 'giving it laldy' with 'The Wee Room Under the Stair' and a monologue by 71-year-old Margaret Burniston. Framed in soft light on the balcony she told simply of her days in her community. Sometimes with laughter and sometimes in tears, the audience saw each banner being given its own moment of glory, and the *pièce de résistance* was December, when Johnnie Bett and Jimmy Chisholm as Widow Twankey and Wishee Washee appeared in full panto rig to perform a specially written 15-minute routine with all the jokes of the project. After mulled wine and speeches, thank you's and flowers, *Keeping Glasgow in Stitches* was launched and as it hung in majesty everyone knew that the effort had been worthwhile.

PANTOMIME
Alastair Cameron

In Glasgow, as in all great cities, there has always been a voracious public appetite for entertainment of any sort. Eighteenth-century records mention visiting shows of jugglers and tumblers, a polar bear which travelled with a bath of water, and a tiger and monkey displayed in the High Street – until the former ate the latter. The monkey had the last laugh, if that is the right phrase, as the tiger choked on the monkey's chain and died.

Gradually, the season for entertainment in the city became concentrated around the Glasgow Fair in July and around the New Year holiday. Until the early years of this century, in common with most of Scotland, Christmas was hardly celebrated in Glasgow. For New Year, the travelling circuses, the touring theatres or geggies, the fairground attractions, the freak shows, the strange tribesmen, the half-men, half-fish and the multicoloured horses which clustered round Glasgow Green in the summer would return for one last outing before shutting up shop for winter.

The first record of a pantomime in Glasgow comes in 1751 when *Harlequin Pantomime or the Dutchman Bitt* was presented at Burrell's Hall just off the Bell of the Brae near the Cathedral. More familiar names start to appear in 1814, when the Theatre Royal, Queen Street, presented *Aladdin*, in which 'no expense in the way of scenic decoration, supernumeraries, Chinese costumes, or stage effects was spared and the result was a complete triumph'. This *Aladdin* was, however, called a melodrama, for pantomime at this time still meant an energetic short piece at the end of the evening's entertainment full of tricks and transformations. It was a much more knock-about and acrobatic form of humour than we are used to now and one which perhaps survives only in the slapstick scenes which are such a feature of present-day pantos.

Pantomimes, as we would recognise them, only began to take shape in Glasgow later in the 19th century. By then the knock-about had become married to a literary script which relied heavily on puns and was written in rhyming couplets. Stirring national sentiments are displayed in this quotation from Rich Waldon's 1916/17 pantomime for the Royal Princess's Theatre, *Tommy Trotter*.

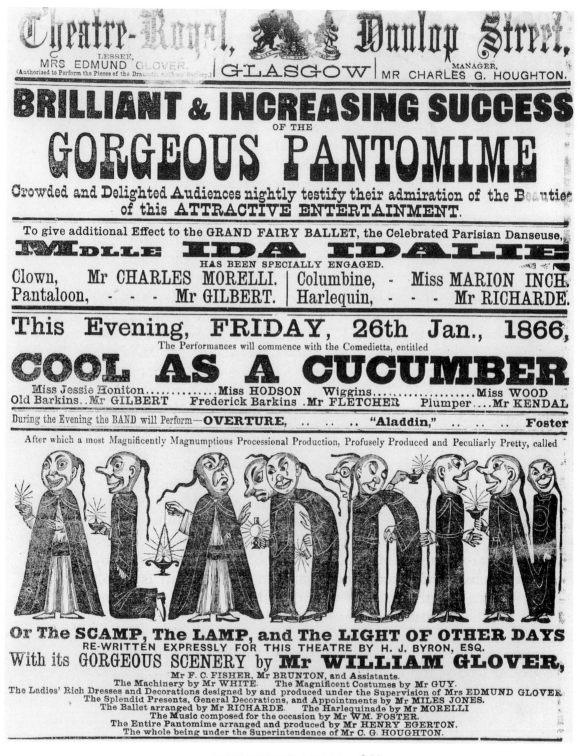

ALADDIN POSTER, JANUARY 1866

This country's fair to look upon, 'tis true;
So is our dear old country Scotland, too,
Worthy of honour, where honour to it is due.
They speak of England's King – we hear the Cockney brag –
The English Navy and the English Flag.
The English Commons and the English Peers
Are daily dinned in our Northern ears.
A little more of loyal Scotland – she has her rights;
In all fierce battles the Scots lad fights.
Good luck to the English, and to the Irish, cheers!
But don't forget the Scottish Highlanders!

In Scotland it wasn't long until Scottish characters were introduced and, following the lead of Walter Scott's novels, it was often the comical characters who were Scots. These pantomimes, which traditionally began on Boxing Day, soon became the way in which the usually sedate theatre companies let their hair down as the actors gleefully sent up their usual roles. Where all the traditions of pantomime, like the Dame – possibly as a result of the example of Dan Leno – being a man in drag and the Principal Boy being a woman with shapely legs – perhaps Madame Vestris? – came from is still a matter of much speculation. But what is clear is that pantomime was a way of making theatre into a money-spinner and that by giving a well-written script to many of the best performers from the variety stage, theatres could ensure full houses for the tricky post-Christmas season. Indeed, the Christmas play for many years subsidised the more serious dramatic efforts of the city. In 1910 the Christmas performances of *Wee MacGreegor* subsidised Ibsen and Chekhov at the Glasgow Repertory Theatre, and in the 1940s it was the turn of the Citizens, having difficulty in establishing themselves in the Gorbals, who were saved by *The Tintock Cup*. This pantomime, which in its first draft is a dull creature indeed, was transformed by an amalgamation of talent, the like of which the Scottish stage has never seen before or since. Stanley Baxter and Duncan McRae, Fulton Mackay, James Gibson and Molly Urquhart transformed the script into a crazy ramble through the Scottish past – with the six Jaimies and Mary Queen of Scots – the Scottish present – with Battlin' Joe McClout, a more irreverent look at Scottish boxing than the Benny Lynch plays of today, and Duncan McRae's Wallflower from the Palais – and the eternal Scotland – the

THE QUIZ ALBUM,
1882

tipsy auntie at New Year, Molly Urquhart's Tatty Bacclante. All these characters entered local lore and the theatre was packed from December till April.

As Glasgow was the centre of the burgeoning Scottish variety stage in the late 19th century, it was inevitable that Glasgow would set the trend for Scottish pantomime. The area round the Saltmarket in the city had seen the first of the country's music-halls and, as these spread from the back rooms of pubs to the purpose-built theatres like the Britannia and the Metropole, so other theatres in the city saw a way to exploit the new and popular performances at least once a year.

Certain of the Glasgow theatres became well known for their pantomimes. Some, such as the Theatre Royal, for the lavishness with which they were mounted, some, like the Alhambra, for the quality of the comedians they used, others, like the Royal Princess's (now the Citizens), for the length and popularity of their shows, and some, like the Queen's at Glasgow Cross, for the vulgarity and hilarity of their performances. But for whatever reason they were known, all the Glasgow theatres were given over to pantomime at Christmas and all could command large audiences. Whether they indulged in the ornate

A WISH FOR JAMIE,
1960

lavishness of the large city-centre theatres or enjoyed the more homely
theatres just outside the fashionable streets, large numbers of Glasgow
citizens went to pantomimes, whether as part of an organised school
treat or in a family group. Christmas pantomimes were – and in many
cases still are – the one show in the year which the majority of the
people go to see.

Why they go is a different matter. For pantomime is all things to
all people. It offers romance, it offers adventure, it offers an exciting
story in which good always triumphs, it offers feats of conjuring skill,
it offers dance, and, above all, it offers laughter, with jokes the audience
understands in accents that they know. It is the most popular, the most
accessible and the most welcoming kind of theatre there is. People who
wouldn't even consider going to a theatre at any other time of the year
know that what they are going to see they will enjoy and understand.

201

STANLEY BAXTER,
ALADDIN, 1986/87

PUSS IN BOOTS,
CITIZENS, 1972/73

Pantomime is also the most flexible of theatrical genres and can accommodate anything from the most recent changes of political leadership to the headlines from that day's newspapers. It is also played for an audience who are welcomed in and not excluded by the performers.

For many, the heyday of pantomime in Glasgow was not the Edwardian era with its lavish shows and casts including, for example, Harry Lauder singing 'I Love a Lassie' and 'Roamin' in the Gloamin'', it was the 1930s. That decade saw the Alhambra and the Pavilion, the Empire and the Theatre Royal rival each other with casts including Dave Willis, Tommy Morgan, Will Fyffe and Harry Gordon. At the Royal Princess's, too, George West was at the height of his fame and all theatres had, in spite of the cinema, a seemingly endless supply of audiences who returned again and again to see their favourite pantomimes.

Like every other form of popular theatre, pantomime went through a bad patch with the introduction of television, but it hit back with the *Wish for Jamie* pantomimes which had casts including Kenneth McKellar, Rikki Fulton and Fay Lenore. The series ran for four years and in one year alone was seen by 250,000 people. However, throughout the '60s there was a feeling that things were not the same, that pantomimes were becoming commercialised and that they were only an excuse to promote television stars. There was also a great deal of comment on the fact that with the 'permissive society' jokes were becoming a little near the knuckle and children were not sufficiently catered for. There were always the Citizens pantomimes like *Tapsellteerio*, though, which always had 13 letters in the title, and for the very young there was Bertha Waddell's children's theatre. These held their own in the midst of a sea of shows which were trying to be modern – and failing.

In Glasgow this trend was broken by Giles Havergal at the Citizens. He promoted traditional literary pantomimes often written by Myles Rodge with a series of gallus Dames, often played by Peter Kelly, and young enthusiastic casts who put new heart into pantomime and new life into the romance ('Jam doughnuts needed jam in them, ham omelettes need ham in them, but not as much as I need you'). In doing so he catered for large numbers of Glaswegians who indirectly subsidised his theatre and who perhaps did not feel confident enough to come to some of his more extravagant productions at other times in

UNA MCLEAN,
ALADDIN, 1986/87

the year. Gradually all theatres in Glasgow went back to traditional entertainment. Now they offer 'proper' pantos with strong story lines and heroes and heroines and Dames played by the likes of Stanley Baxter, Rikki Fulton, Johnny Beattie, Andy Cameron, Walter Carr and Jimmy Logan, often supported magnificently by Una McLean.

Pantomime at Christmas is an experience which almost all the people in the city share – even though they last way beyond Ne'erday. Theatre in Scotland needs pantomimes to survive. They are more than just nostalgia; we all need to go on being made to laugh and sigh, to be amazed, to be allowed to dream, to shout out and to cry in public, even if it is only once a year. Panto is magic.

Left
WALTER CARR,
ALADDIN, 1986/87

IN MAY 1991 THE BANNERS TRAVELLED
TO ROSTOV-ON-DON AS PART OF A
TWINNING EVENT. INSPIRED BY *KEEPING
GLASGOW IN STITCHES*, 150 RUSSIAN
WOMEN WORKED IN SECRET FOR FIVE
DAYS AND NIGHTS TO MAKE THIS
BANNER. COMPLETE WITH WONDERFUL
DETAILS OF GLASGOW PIPERS AND DON
COSSACKS, IT DEMONSTRATES THE SKILL
AND HUMOUR OF THE ROSTOVITES.
GIVEN AS A GIFT TO THE PEOPLE OF
GLASGOW IT IS A MOVING SYMBOL OF
FRIENDSHIP.

THE PARTICIPANTS

Arma Abdullah
Reeah Abercrombie
Georgina Abernethy
Marion Acteson
Agnes Affleck
Sam Ainslie
Gillian Aitken
Gazalla Akram
Dorothy Allan
Jamie Allan
Flora Allen
Irene Alston
Lucy Andrew
Helen Andrew
Dianna Andrews
Pony Angorro
Jennifer Arnold
Joanne Arnold
Shazia Ashraf
Christine Aston
Annette Bailey
Laura Baillie
Nancy Baillie-Scott
Sheila Bain
Helen Bak
Muriel H. Baker
David Balfour
Henrietta Banks
Cathie Barclay
Rhonda Barclay
Evi Barlow
May Barnsdale
Alan Barr
Ellen Barr
Rhoda Barr
Andrew Barret
Jonathan Barret
Margaret Barrie
Isobel Barrie
Monica Beale
Margaret Beattie
Daniel Beggs
Dorothy Bell
Morag Bell
Eileen Bellamy
Anthony Bennett
Mary Bennis
Huck Bergius
Christine Berry
Daphne Bertie
Johnnie Bett
M. Beveridge
Mrs Birrell
Carol Birss
Mark Blair
Rosemary Boney
Samira Bouday
Nicola Boyle
Scott Brannan

Susan Brattin
Gill Brooks
Alison Brown
Jill Brown
Margaret Brown
Pat Brown
Bob Brown
Annette Browning
Mary Bruce
Bunty Bryson
Janey Buchan
Norman Buchan
Betty Buchanan
Ross Buchanan
Anthony Burnett
Margaret Burniston
Nicky Burns
Mary Ann Burrow
Lexie Burrows
Margaret Byars
Nan Byron
Marilyn Caddell
Deborah Calder
Mrs M. Caldow
Gillian Caldwell
Jennifer Caldwell
E. Cameron
Eileen Cameron
Netta Cameron
Jenny Campbell
Jamie Campbell
E. Campbell
Elizabeth Campbell
Fiona Campbell
Joyce Campbell
Margaret Campbell
Molly Campbell
Mrs Jane Campbell-Smith
Catherine Canavan
Graham Carroll
Jane Carroll
Sadie Cassells
Bel Caven
Alister Chan
Fareed Cheema
Jimmy Chisolm
Atia Chowdhury
Nihar Chowdhury
Marjinder Chung
Marion Clancy
Kathleen Clark
Gary Clark
Mrs M. M. Clark
Dorothy Clelland
Catherine Close
Rebecca Close
Marie Cocozza
Sarah Cochrane
Rebecca Cochrane

Rosemary Condie
R. C. Connal
Valerie Cooke
Ian Cooney
Belinda Corbett
Sine Cormack
Frances Coull
Jean Cowie
Judith Cowley
Josephine Cox
Corinne Craig
Sheila Crawford
Ann Crawley
June Crisfield Chapman
Beth Cross
Fiona Crowe
Tim Cullen
Elaine Cunningham
Liz Cunningham
Hilary Cusker
Christine Cutt
M. Dalgleish
John Danielewski
Ann Danielson
John Davidson
Mattie Davidson
Joseph Davie
Christopher Davies
Lorraine Davin
Christine Davis
Catherine Dawson
Janet Dawson
Diana Desport
Robin Dickie
Betty Dickson
Billy Differ
Emma Docherty
Mary Donachie
Charlotte Donaldson
Emily Donaldson
Michael Donnelly
Iain Douglas
Margaret Downie
Leanne Duddy
Joyce Duguid
Etta Dunbar
Katie Durie
Mary Duxbury
M. Dykes
Andrew Eastcroft
Helen Eastcroft
Leslie Evans
Felicity Evans
May Evans
Mrs Evans
Marcella Evaristi
Diana Fairlie
Elizabeth Fairlie
Joanna Fairlie

Nina Faith
Margaret Falconer
Simon Fanshawe
Ellen Farrell
Jacqueline Farrell
Avril Fearns
Hilary Fearns
Christine Felly
Helen P. Fergus
Anna Ferguson
Janet Ferrol
Lucille Fleming
Betty Fleming
Elizabeth Fleming
Jenny Fleming
Hilary Forster
Edith Frame
Barrie Frame
Jason Frame
Mary Frame
Jane Fraser
Risha Freedmen
Isabel French
Hannah Frew-Paterson
Bob Fullerton
Nan Fyfe
A. Gallacher
Catherine Gallacher
Betty Galt
Brij Gandhi
Prof David George
Mrs Ghai
Marie Gibbs
Mrs M. Gibson
Rose Gillan
Mrs Anna Gillen
May Gillon
Mrs M. Gillon
Kevin Gillespie
Isabel Girvan
Margaret Goodall
Margaret Goodrick
Chris Gordon
Val Graham
Alasdair Graham
Catherine Graham
Alex Graham
Maggie Grant
Catherine Grassie
Emma Gray
Dorothy Green
Natalie Green
Vicki Green
Peggy Gregory
Audrey Groom
Asheesh Gupta
Allie Hall
Carsi Hall
P. Haman

Ann Hamilton
Ada Hamilton
Gordon Hamilton
Phyllis Hardie
Sarah Harper
Alison Harper
Kate Harvey
Marda Hasler
Andrew Hay
Betty Hayton
Carey Henderson
Johanna Henderson
Daniel Hecht
Graeme Henderson
Veronica Heinney
Margaret Hill
Pat Hillhouse
Hilary Hiram
Jean Hogg
Joanna Holmes
Harsharyn Hooryn
Stuart Hopps
M. Horne
Eleanor Horsman
Susan Horsman
Elaine Hosie
Gillian Hosie
Jenny Hosie
Pat Hossack
E. Hough
Christopher Houston
Laura Houston
Gayle Houstoun
Nanette Hotchkiss
Margaret Howie
Marjorie Howie
Claudia Hughes
Janice Hughes
Gail Hughes
Chris Hunter
Margo Hunter
Morag Hunter
A. Inglis
Victoria Ingram
Alison Irwin
Sandra Jack
John Jackson
Nazreen Jamil
Shebeen Jamil
Anurag Jodhawat
Grace Johannsen
Peggy Johnston
Rheina Johnston
Bessie Johnstone
Elizabeth Johnstone
Rachael Johnstone
Betty Jolly
Mrs Jolliffe
Debbie Jones

Beena Joshi
Stephen Kay
J. Keady
Richard Keir
Jinty Kerr
Teresa Kerr
Shujaat Khan
Sandi Kielhmann
Morag Kilpatrick
E. King
Elspeth King
Gareth King
Beverley Kirk
V. Kirkwood
Muriel Kitchener
Hardrig Krasinka
Martin Lacy
Kitty Laidlaw
Jo Lamb
M. Lang
Ross Lang
Nancy Langan
Mrs L. Law
Calum Lawson
Jean Leader
Lynette Learmont
M. Leat
Andrea Lee
Jean Leggat
Margaret Leggat
Janet Leitch
Caroline Levett
Christina Levy
S. Leitch
Mrs D. Lewis
D. Lindsay
Christine Linnell
Frank Little
Ann Livingston
Liz Lochhead
Malcolm Lochhead
Elizabeth Lorio
Elizabeth Lothian
M. Lynch
Clara Lyttle
Jean Mabon
Sheena MacBryde
Marianne MacBryde
Flora MacDonald
Fergus MacDonald
Jean MacGregor
Bob Macaulay
Christine Macaulay
Anna Macdonald
Jean Macdonald
Hazel Macdonald
Tove Macdonald
John Macenhill
Lynne Mack

207

Bill Mackay
E. Mackay
Jenny Mackay
Pat Mackay
Rona Mackie
Sara Mackinnon
John Major
Stephen Mallan
Rona Malcolm
Bessie Maclaren
Ann Maclean
Lyn Macmartin
Dorothy Makin
Fraser Mann
Magdalene Manning
Christopher Manson
Christine Manzie
Peter Marco
Corona Marshall
Meg Marshall
Mrs E. M. Marshall
Hilda Marshall
Marion Marshall
Mary Marshall
Grace Martin
Mary Mason
Sheena Masson
Manjula Math
Stuart Mathieson
Veronica Matthew
Michelle McAulay
Isobel McAvoy
A. M. McCallum
Alastair McCallum
Francesca McCarron
Helen McCart
Lorna McCarthy
W. McCormack
Elizabeth McCormick
Nancy McAlpine
Janet McBain
Ann McCaig
Wendy McCallum
Andrew McCallum
Mary McCarron
Nancy McCarty
Linda McClarkin
Anne McColl
Malcolm McCormick
Elizabeth McCormick
John McCrimmon
Norma McCrone
Elizabeth McCulloch
Martin McDonald
Janet McDiarmid
John McEwan
Donna McFadden
Lex McFadyen
Renee McFedris
Kelly McGeachy

Brian McGeoch
Elizabeth McGettigan
Alison McGlashan
Margaret McGourty
Anna McGowan
Peter McGowan
Lorainne McGregor
Rosalyn McGregor
Sheena McGregor
Antoinette McGurl
Karen McIlhinney
J. McIntyre
Pam McIntyre
Fiona McIvor
Heather McKenna
Annie McKenzie
Janet McKenzie
Mary McKenzie
Flora McKerrell
Grace McKinnon
Bessie McLaren
Isobel McLay
Judith McLay
Bill McLean
I. McLeod
Margaret McLellan
F. McMahon
Debbie McMillan
Martha McMillan
Lousia McMinn
Alison McMorland
Helen McNeil
Maureen McNicol
Mrs S. P. McNidder
Jill McOwatt
Jamie McPherson
John McPherson
Sharon McPhun
Margaret McSporran
David McTaggart
Ewan McVicar
Bhadra Meatha
Doris Meek
Helen Millar
Linda Millcoat
Ann Marie Miller
David Miller
Hazel Miller
Elizabeth Miller
J. Milne
Audrey Minto
Irene Mitchell
Raymond Mitchell
Sabrina Mohammed
Jacques Moine
Irene Morland
Agnes Morrison
Claire Morrison
Julie Morrison
Jean Morrison

Isabel Morrison
Mrs I. C. Moule
Fariedha Muhammed
Evylyn Muir
Catriona Muir
Mary Muir
Agnes Mulholland
Anne Mundie
Sarah Munro
Janice Murphy
Peter Murphy
Anna Murray
Betty Murray
Helen Murray
Laxmi Murti
Fay Neilly
Sonia Newman
Margaret Nisbet
Derek Niven
Fathema Noor
Salma Noor
Andrew Nuffallum
Phil O'Brian
C. O'Donnell
Jeanette O'Donnell
Dr P. J. O'Dwyer
Mark O'Neill
May O'Neil
Mavis Oldham
George Oomen
Jason Orr
Rachael Owen
Eleanor Oxburgh
Jean Parker
Miss N. Pate
Kim Paterson
Miss D. M. Paterson
Claire Paterson
Lynne Paterson
Dorothy Paton
Shiela Paton
D. Patoy
Noreen Patrick
Susie Patrick
David Peace
Derek Pearce
Ann Petrie
B. Pinkerston
Helen Pollock
Anna Pomfret
Terry Porter
Christopher Pothan
Nana Poustie
Rose Proden
Sharon Prendergast
Andre Prost
Anna Purdie
Joseph Quail
Mary Quinn
Mae Quinn

Edith Rabento
Nell Rae
Elisabeth Ramage
Liz Ramsay
Jess Ramsay
Yasmeen Razag
Trevor Rees
Roderick Reid
Elayne Reilley
C. Relley
David Rennie
Maureen Rennie
Mrs C. Rettig
Stacia Rice
Margaret Richards
Lindi Richardson
Gary Riordan
Barry Ritchie
Eliana Ritchie
Christian Robert
Leigh Roberts
Sheila Robertson
Mrs H. Robertson
Helen Robins
Mary Robins
Mary Robinson
Pat Rodger
Marilyn Rooney
Isabel Ross
Anne Ross
Molly Ross
Kate Ross
Christopher Roushias
Miss J. Rutherford
Kenneth Ryan
Scott Rybarczky
Francois Rysto
Rehana Sadiq
Wendy Sandiford
Nahar Sayed
Wendy Scobie
Amanda Scott
D. Scott
Margaret Scott
Anne Scott
Janette Scullion
Jeannette Semple
Mrs Shanks
Margaret Shannon
Isobel Shaw
Lindsay Shaw
Claire Sharp
Barbara Shepherd
Blodwen Shill
Chandra Shrestha
Ashley Sime
Jean Singleton
Harry Slade
Billy Sloan
Sandra Sloman

Pat Sloss
Elaine Smernicki
J. R. Smith
Ann Smith
Grace Smith
Jacqueline Smith
Mairead Smith
M. Smith
Stephen Smith
Isabel Smyth
Margaret Smyth
Margaret Smyth
Julian Spalding
Hilary Speed
Leena Speirs
Natalie Spurr
Rebecca Spurr
Dorothy Stalker
Catherine Stark
Josephine Stewart
Josephine Stewart
Kirsten Stewart
Margaret Stewart
Steven Stewart
Mary Stirling
N. Stiven
Ruth Storie
Vivian Strang
Gill Strathie
Sarah Struthers
Sarah Sumsion
Dorothy Sutherland
Heather Sutherland
Maureen Swan
Morven Swan
Imran Tabraiz
Elizabeth Tait
Sue Tait
Miss D. Tait
Jean Taylor
Mrs P. Taylor
Sheena Taylor
Yvette Taylor
Margaret Telfer
Marie Telfer
William Telfer
Amanda Thompson
Barbara Thompson
Eiv Thomson
Helen Thomson
Margaret Thomson
Morag Thomson
Tracy Thomson
Ann Traycik
Janice Trewinnard
Daye Tucker
Anna Tulloch
Jean Turkington
Mary Ann Turley
Craig Turner

Shaniece Ullah
Jaya Varma
Hausa Varma
Elizabeth Waddell
Sandra Waddell
Barbara Walker
Shiela Walker
Lorna Wallace
Susan Wallace
Naomi Walls
Rosemary Walls
Ann Ward
Thomas Ward
Catherine Waterson
Mavourneen Watkins
Betty Watson
Margaret Watson
Claire Watters
James Weeks
Doreen West
Marion White
M. E. Whiteley
Grace Whitelock
Robert Whiteside
Mrs S. Whitmire
Susan Whittaker
Joyce Whittick
Mrs M. Whyte
M. Wight
Jonnie Wilkes
Margaret Wilkes
June Wilkie
Kathy Wilkinson
Mary Wilkinson
Isabel Williams
Suad Wak Williams
Catherine Wills
Elma Wilson
Lysbeth Wilson
Patricia Wilson
Senga Wilson
Andy Wong
Chi-Wing Wong
William Wong
Derek Wood
Irene Woods
Betty Workman
Catherine Workman
Debbie Wright
Agnes Wylie
Mampta Yadau
Edith Yeoman
Mary Yorston
Jean Young
Thelma Youngson
Khalda Yousef
Izra Zaater
Islam Zaater
Samer Zaater
Sawson Zaater
Margaret Zmijewski

This list is as complete as we can make it. However, in a project of this size, some names could have been left out, either because the person forgot to sign the register or because we could just not read their handwriting. To those people, if any, we apologise and hope you will understand.